NO EASY
RIDE

REFLECTIONS
ON MY LIFE
IN THE RCMP

IAN T. PARSONS

VICTORIA · VANCOUVER · CALGARY

Heritage House Publishing Company Ltd.
heritagehouse.ca

LIBRARY AND ARCHIVES CANADA CATALOGUING IN PUBLICATION

Parsons, Ian T.
    No easy ride: reflections on my life in the RCMP / Ian T. Parsons.

Issued also in electronic formats.
ISBN 978-1-927527-16-0

1. Parsons, Ian T. 2. Royal Canadian Mounted Police—Biography.
I. Title.

HV7911.P36A3 2013   363.2092   C2013-900025-9

Edited by Lesley Reynolds
Copyedited by Lara Kordic
Proofread by Lesley Cameron
Cover and book design by Jacqui Thomas
Cover photo (top) by Pamela Mills. Dedicated in memory of her father, RCMP Staff/
    Sgt. Gerald (Gerry) F. Mills; cover photo (bottom) by Savushkin/iStockphoto.com

 The interior of this book was produced on 30% post-consumer recycled
paper, processed chlorine free and printed with vegetable-based inks.

Heritage House acknowledges the financial support for its publishing program from the
Government of Canada through the Canada Book Fund (CBF), Canada Council for the
Arts and the province of British Columbia through the British Columbia Arts Council
and the Book Publishing Tax Credit.

17 16 15 14 13 1 2 3 4 5

Printed in Canada

---

*Dedicated to the two most
important women in my life:
my wife, Lynne, and my daughter, Michelle.
The world is a better place for your intellect,
compassion and common sense.
Also to my mother, Patricia Parsons,
who devoted 60 years to supporting
her husband and her son in their
RCMP careers. She passed away in
October 2012 in her 102nd year.*

CONTENTS

PUBLISHER'S FOREWORD

It has long been the legacy and legend of the Royal Canadian Mounted Police (RCMP), Canada's national police force, that they could overcome any obstacle when asked to do too much with too little. It was a cherished reputation built over a century of policing new frontiers, at first across the Canadian prairie and later over the 3,000 miles from Vancouver Island to Newfoundland. These brave men usually functioned alone, remote from media scrutiny and without the many complexities of modern times. Through real deeds and, later, Hollywood portrayals, the police force established an image that became an internationally recognized symbol of Canadian society and justice. Today, maintaining that reputation is proving burdensome.

Canada's parliament first passed a bill in 1873 to create the North West Mounted Police (NWMP) and establish a force of 300 scarlet-coated riders, sent west from Ontario with a mandate to bring law and order to the Dominion's North-West Territories. Things started badly.

Most historians agree that the NWMP's first commissioner was the wrong leader on the wrong trail with the wrong horses. During the 10 weeks after disembarking the Red River camp at Fort Dufferin on July 8, 1874, Colonel George French failed dismally, forcing his ill-conceived strategy on what started as six divisions of 50 mounted policemen. Even as they broke camp that day, two of French's division leaders resigned in total frustration, angered that their commissioner insisted on using his regal hand-picked eastern steeds instead of trained cart horses readily available at the fort.

Within 60 days, almost three-quarters of French's herd of matching bays, light bays, chestnuts, blacks, browns and greys were either dead or lame. Supplies had dwindled, morale was on its own death march and they were effectively lost. The threat of early snow and even starvation hung over the camp as French and his assistant commissioner, James Macleod, headed south into Montana in search of supplies and a good scout.

Fortunately the weather held and supplies were secured, and as a blessing to all, George French was summoned east by his superiors. With the well-respected Macleod left in charge and their new scout, Jerry Potts, at the front of their column, the NWMP headed farther west to build their first fort and establish a foothold for law and order on the Canadian prairie at Fort Macleod.

In contrast to the bloodletting that occurred on American soil, the NWMP gained the trust of tribal leaders and maintained peace through their first decade in the West. In 1886, after the Metis rebellion, there were 1,000 men enlisted, and the achievements of James Macleod, Sam Steele, James Walsh, Cecil Denny, other NWMP original recruits and Jerry Potts are now well documented.

In spite of their heroics, the Mounties' existence was threatened in 1896 when Prime Minister Wilfrid Laurier announced his intent to disband the NWMP. A strong protest from the West and the beginnings of the chaotic Klondike gold rush assured the survival of the Force and its expansion into the Yukon. There, in gold camps north of Whitehorse, tiny detachments kept law and order, as they had done when small patrols had chased off Montana whisky traders, ridden in peace among the villages of the Blackfoot Confederacy, greeted the arrival of Sitting Bull and his followers as he crossed the Medicine

Line, maintained peace as gangs of navvies built the rail lines to the mountains and protected ranchers and settlers as they set out to tame a raw landscape.

The NWMP became the Royal Northwest Mounted Police (RNWMP) by a proclamation of King Edward VII in 1904. When the provinces of Alberta and Saskatchewan were formed the following year, the RNWMP continued to maintain both provincial law and federal law in the lands that were their first arena. That role continued until 1917, when both Saskatchewan and Alberta established their own provincial police forces, as British Columbia had done decades before. The following year the RNWMP was also assigned duties to handle federal laws in BC, a jurisdiction already well served provincially.

Even before there was a Canada, the colonies of Vancouver Island and British Columbia shared early policing roots that dated back to the 1858 Fraser River and Cariboo gold rushes. When BC entered Confederation in 1871, the British Columbia Constabulary was formed. In 1895 the name was changed to the BC Provincial Police (BCPP). The BCPP would remain the prominent West Coast police presence through the Second World War and the early post-war years. At its peak, it was in charge of all rural areas plus 40 municipalities throughout the province.

Through the First World War, the RNWMP was largely confined to the Prairie provinces and Yukon Territory. East of Manitoba, federal policing had long been handled by the Dominion Police Force, a body originally formed five years before the NWMP to protect Ottawa politicians from assassination attempts. The Dominion force gradually expanded to administer federal laws, including a national fingerprint bureau and the parole service, and served as protector of naval dockyards at Halifax and Esquimalt, near Victoria, BC. It also assumed various policing duties in the Maritime provinces until the end of the Great War, when its contingent of almost 1,000 was briefly made a civilian arm of the Canadian Military Police Corps.

In 1920, the merging of the western-based RNWMP with the civilian corps of the Canadian Military Police Corps finally resulted in a truly national police force. The prominent red serge of the Mounties became the official uniform of the Royal Canadian Mounted Police, and the force was well on its way to building the most complex infrastructure of any police body in the world.

Establishing detachments in the High Arctic soon became a priority to protect Canadian sovereignty. By 1928, the Force had returned to handling Saskatchewan's provincial laws under contract. Four years later, as the Depression stirred civilian unrest, members signed contracts with Manitoba and the three Maritime provinces to act as their provincial police as well. They also took over federal policing along Canada's coastal perimeter while absorbing personnel and vessels from the Preventive Service of the Department of National Revenue. The essence of the RCMP Marine Section would be defined a decade later by Sergeant Henry Larsen, who captained the schooner *St. Roch* as it carved its way through the ice-laden Northwest Passage and became the first ship to ever circumnavigate North America.

In 1950, new layers of complexity were built into the RCMP when they were contracted as the provincial force in Canada's newest province of Newfoundland, while absorbing the country's oldest police roots when they integrated the BC Provincial Police into their structure. They were now the dominant municipal, provincial and federal police agency in Western Canada.

It was into this era of policing that Ian T. Parsons was born. His father, Joseph, had been a proud member of the RCMP since 1930. Ian enlisted while his father was still active in the Force, becoming part of a tandem that would serve their country for 64 consecutive years.

In the 33 years that Ian Parsons served, his assignments took him across the country from St. John's, Newfoundland, to a final posting on Vancouver Island. He entered the Force while "old-school" training procedures were still in play. Later, as a new philosophy permeated the Force, he returned to teach at Regina in classrooms occupied by both men and women and enlistees representing many cultures. But Ian Parsons not only taught raw recruits in Regina; while stationed at headquarters in Ottawa, he also lectured the old guard of sometimes resistant RCMP senior officers on the adoption of new ways, new techniques and new social pressures of political correctness.

Outside of his stint in Ottawa, most of Ian Parsons's career was spent in rural detachments where RCMP members were most often a respected part of a close community. The diversity of his postings brought him in touch with all aspects of policing, including highway patrol, provincial issues and First Nations law enforcement. For his final posting, he was the operational officer and assistant officer commanding on Vancouver Island, a component of the single most complex division in the RCMP.

By the time he retired with the rank of inspector, Parsons had a policeman's trunk full of colourful stories, insightful observations and amusing yarns that he now shares in this memoir. They provide an entertaining backdrop for his candid assessment of things gone wrong in the Force.

In retirement, Parsons has remained active amongst his peers but also independent in his thinking. In recent years, as his beloved Force has faced crisis after crisis Ian Parsons has built his own thesis on how to fix things. He is now willing to speak out and try to help fix what so many Canadians feel is broken. For this ex-Mountie, it is more than gender issues, bad judgements and use of excessive force, unwieldy discipline procedures and low morale. It is about a structure and a mandate far too complex and fundamentally unfixable. Now distant enough from the inside to see both the trees and the forest, Inspector I.T. Parsons (Retired) offers a solution.

Rodger Touchie

PREFACE

The man who lived in my house—my father—had a thundering voice and seemed six foot seventeen. He was a fabled law-enforcement officer and a survivor of gunfights. I was raised in an RCMP family and will forever carry great affection for the Royal Red; it is part of my DNA. My earliest memories are of a forest of high brown boots, the sound of men's voices and the smell of tobacco and occasionally beer wafting through our home. My father was at the core of this boisterous regiment, an alpha male among men who were held in high esteem in the communities where we lived. Police cars, firearms, police dogs, uniforms—these awe-inspiring and intimidating tools and trappings of law enforcement were a part of the everyday routine of family life. Even when my father's lofty height seemed to diminish as I became a rebellious teenager, his stature as a hero never faded. He left an indelible impression on me and inspired me to follow my own career in the RCMP.

Over 33 years with the RCMP, I served from sea to sea, including postings in several provinces. While all the events I recount in these pages are authentic, they are viewed through perceptions and opinions acquired over a lifetime. In telling my story, I have changed the names of some people and places for reasons of confidentiality, and on rare occasions I have altered incidents or fictionalized characters to enhance the flow of the work. Some incidents are composites of several separate scenarios and as such cannot be attributed to specific individuals. The reader will hear a recruit, an investigator, a researcher, a manager and perhaps even a philosopher as I progress through the stages of my law-enforcement career.

Much of my story occurred prior to the 1970s, a decade when a maelstrom of change descended upon not just the RCMP, but our entire world. Many RCMP veterans define the period from the inception of the Force in 1873 to the late 1960s as "the Golden Era." The "golden" aspect most probably alludes to the impeccable external reputation of the Force, seemingly untarnished by assorted mischief committed by those inside the organization during those halcyon years. Symbolic of the end of this era, equitation was removed from RCMP training in 1966. The Regina stables were closed and all things equine moved to "N" Division Rockcliffe, in Ottawa, Ontario. The demise of equitation training coincided with the beginning of an amazing organizational transformation. The RCMP has had to cope with sweeping changes, including new technology, compensation for overtime work, women in policing, acquisition of support staff and the right to challenge management through representation. As is often the case, even these positive changes have been disruptive and frequently unwelcome.

My reasons for writing this book are twofold. While I hope my story entertains readers and provides a window into the everyday challenges that faced RCMP members during the past few decades, I also wish to share my concerns for the future of the Force. The RCMP evolved from a small band of men in 1873 into a viable police organization during the early part of the 20th century. Initial frontier police duties demanded little sophistication, but the Force acquired expertise as it grew and assumed responsibility for almost all policing functions in the dominion of Canada. As demands on the RCMP increased, it was unable to stay abreast of this astounding growth, largely due to its high recruiting standards and limited training facilities. The philosophy of the RCMP has always been "never say no." This inability to decline a request is at the root of many of the organization's problems. I strongly believe that the Force must shed some of its numerous and varied burdens if it hopes to survive as the charismatic institution beloved by so many Canadians.

CHAPTER ONE

THE WAY IT WAS

There is little chance that my career in the RCMP would ever have happened without my father's example. Like many young immigrants of his era, he sought a new life in Canada and worked through adversity to build a successful career. But his story is also a snapshot of the RCMP during the years it grew to become a four-tiered organization. It happened during Canada's adolescence as a country, when it was largely populated by white Anglo-Saxon Protestants and Catholics. With the exception of Quebec, Canada's laws and mores were almost exclusively British.

In 1922 my father, 16-year-old Joseph Thomas Parsons, embarked on an arduous ocean voyage across the Atlantic. His long journey by sea and over land concluded in Regina, Saskatchewan. His elder brother, who had already immigrated to Canada, had told him of an employment opportunity with a grain farmer. Joseph left Cornwall, England, and the oppression of stern Methodist parents and set out to seek his fortune in Canada. He arrived in a prosperous new land, finding ample work as a farm labourer and earning good money. He dreamed of buying land for his own farm, and, acting on advice, he invested all of his earnings in the stock market. The future looked extremely promising until he lost his nest egg in the 1929 worldwide stock market crash. With few options available to him, he learned the RCMP was hiring able-bodied young men to police the Canadian west. He applied and was accepted in 1930. Upon completion of his training, he was posted to Kelvington, a small farming community in Saskatchewan.

After only two years' service, Joseph became involved in an investigation and manhunt that would set his destiny in the Force. The account of the incident below is based on an article by Henry M. Savage that was originally published in the Regina *Leader Post* in 1944 and later reprinted in the *RCMP Quarterly*.

In June and July of 1932, a crime wave occurred in the Yorkton, Saskatchewan, area. Someone was robbing hardware stores and gas stations in small towns in the region, and the RCMP was having no luck in finding the culprits. It was particularly troubling since the thieves had stolen firearms and large quantities of ammunition in several of these burglaries. The only clue was the presence of a blue sedan in the area of several of the offences.

On the night of July 4, Constable M.V. Novakowski of the RCMP detachment at Yorkton was patrolling the rainy highway about 20 miles west of Yorkton, stopping vehicles and questioning occupants. As he stood on the road and tried to wave down an approaching dark blue sedan, it accelerated, forcing him to jump out of the way, and sped off. Novakowski got into his police car and took off in pursuit of the fleeing vehicle. They sped along for miles, through the little town of Theodore and beyond. At one point the fleeing vehicle's door opened and Novakowski thought he heard a bullet whistle past his car window. After chasing the car unsuccessfully for 20 miles, Novakowski abandoned the chase at Sheho and phoned ahead to Foam Lake, the next police detachment.

Constable Novakowski spoke with Corporal Leonard Victor Ralls and explained that the suspect car was heading his way. Ralls assured Novakowski that he would attempt to intercept it. A short time later, west of Foam Lake, a series of explosions near the farm home of

Mr. and Mrs. Alex Baird awakened the couple. Alex looked out and saw a car driving away to the east and heard two more explosions. He also heard a weak call for help and hurried outside to find Corporal Ralls mortally wounded. Ralls died en route to the doctor. The Yorkton RCMP detachment was told of the murder, and an all-points bulletin went out across the province. In less than an hour 40, RCMP members rallied to block all highways in the district. A private aircraft was also launched for the search.

At the murder scene, Corporal Ralls's police car was found in the ditch with the ignition wires severed. There were tire tracks from another vehicle that appeared to be equipped with Goodyear tires. Not far from the police car, Ralls's .45 calibre police revolver was found with two live and two discharged shells. The offending vehicle had turned off the highway east of Foam Lake and seemed to be heading north through very rough country. Members gave chase, but it had rained steadily for three days and their cars became mired up to the fender wells with mud. Nevertheless, they moved steadily northward through the thick bush country as dawn broke.

At about noon, near the village of Lintlaw and 90 miles north of Foam Lake, police found a blue Plymouth abandoned and covered with mud. The windshield and rear windows were missing, and four bullets had struck the car in the hood area. The vehicle had been stolen from a garage in Zealandia on the night of June 12. Mounted policemen travelling by horse, railway jiggers and car continued the hunt through the next night. Early Wednesday morning, they received word that three men, one carrying a rifle, had visited a local farm the previous evening. They had demanded a meal and left in a westerly direction through the bush. Later that day, some school children saw them running across a road. More tips came in, but it seemed the RCMP were always minutes behind the trio.

The next morning, the three men stopped at a farm and again demanded a meal. They then fled with four horses, apparently heading for the Greenwater Lake timber reserve, where it would become extremely difficult to track and capture them. A command centre was established at Kelvington, a small farming community with a two-man detachment. The junior man was my father, Constable Joe Parsons, who had barely two years' service. Up to this point, his law-enforcement experience consisted of investigating minor thefts, the odd family squabble and the occasional disturbance initiated by too much liquor. Now conscripted into the manhunt for the killers of a police officer, his level of anxiety was palpable. More than 30 police officers and over 200 armed civilians were now focused on capturing the fugitives and were traversing muskeg and bog, felling trees and moving through mud holes. Many cars became damaged beyond repair. As night fell again, paranoia ruled and isolated residents took refuge with neighbours.

About noon on Thursday, while a blazing sun shone overhead, my father and town constable Wilson Hayes of Wadena walked into a clearing in the bush and discovered three horses tethered to a tree. A short distance away was a farmhouse. It immediately occurred to my father that the killers had stopped once again for a meal. The two policemen moved back into the bush and waited for the men to appear. Soon a man wearing overalls, a smock and a cap came out of the house and walked toward them. When he neared, my father leapt out, levelled his .45 Colt revolver at the stranger and commanded, "Freeze!" For an instant, the stranger stared at the policeman in astonishment. Then, wheeling about to cry in alarm, he ran for the house. He had not gone far when my father overtook him, threw him to the ground and handcuffed him. The man struggled and tried to warn his partners, so my father knocked him unconscious to quiet him. He then turned his prisoner over to Hayes and told him to take the man into the bush while he faced the other two gunmen alone. The other two had heard the disturbance and dashed from the dwelling in the direction of the horses. They gasped in surprise when they spotted my father, who again shouted, "Freeze!" The men drew revolvers and a volley of shots was exchanged before the pair rushed into the heavy brush in different directions. It was later determined that one of them had been severely wounded by my father's return fire.

Soon all the searchers converged on the scene and began to scour the surrounding bush, while the captured man was interrogated. Finally breaking down, he identified himself as Mike Kuralak and gave a full confession about his part in the robberies and murder of Corporal Ralls. He implicated his brother, Bill, and a man named Bill Miller, who had just been released from prison. Miller was the leader and apparently the one who had murdered Corporal Ralls.

Police were closing in on the remaining fugitives and discovered early the following morning that one of them had gone to ground at another farm home. They surrounded the house and then entered to find Bill Kuralak asleep, fully clothed and with a loaded revolver under his pillow. When police found Miller later that morning, he was riding on a wagon and disguised as a teamster. When he realized he'd been discovered, he leapt from the wagon and fled into the bush. As a cordon of police closed in on him, a shot was heard. When they found his body, there was a self-inflicted bullet wound in his right temple. Further examination revealed a smashed bone above the ankle of his right leg and a gaping wound in his abdomen, believed to be from the gunfight with my father. Investigators were astounded at Miller's stamina, given the severity of his injuries.

The work of the RCMP was just beginning, as they had to prepare for the trial of the Kuralaks. Thanks to some excellent forensic work, the weapons carried by the three accused were directly linked to the death of Corporal Ralls. During the trial, my father was vigorously cross-examined. Defence counsel suggested that he had brutalized his prisoner by knocking him unconscious during the arrest; however, the court concluded that he had only used as much force as was reasonably necessary, as Mike Kuralak had to be prevented from warning his partners. Bill Kuralak, the clean-cut, 23-year-old gunman, was found guilty and sentenced to be hanged in Regina on December 29, 1932. His 17-year-old brother, Mike, was convicted of manslaughter and sentenced to 15 years in Prince Albert Penitentiary.

My father's heroic actions earned him much attention and eventual early promotion. He remained in Kelvington, and it was not long before he distinguished himself in several other high-profile cases. He received his first detachment command at Kamsack, Saskatchewan. In the meantime he met an attractive red-headed nurse named Mary Violet Patricia McNamee, and—after a lengthy courtship while awaiting permission from the Force to marry—they were wed in 1937. I was born in Kamsack in 1940, and my sister JoAnne arrived two years later. (My youngest sister, Shari, came along 16 years later.) Dad became the detachment commander at Pelly, Saskatchewan, and moved to Yorkton in 1944 for a promotion to sergeant. By 1950 he had 20 years' service and held the rank of staff sergeant.

As a child, I loved everything about my father's office in Yorkton and would often go there. I guess I was considered somewhat precocious, and when I occasionally became a nuisance he would shoo me home. One day, when I was about 11 years of age, two of the plainclothes members were going out for a drive, and my father asked them to take me along to get me out of his hair. It was the dead of winter and I rode in the back seat. I knew both of these chaps and often bantered with them. I warned them to watch out because my dad was "the boss of them," implying that these constables had to defer to me. They pulled the car over. There were no buildings, just bald prairie and snow. They commanded me to get out of the car, and when I did as they said they drove away, leaving me on the side of the road in –20°F weather. I could see the snow billowing up from the car as they disappeared. I felt totally abandoned. Just as I was starting to panic, the two drove up. They rolled the window down and wanted to know if I was going to behave. I told them I would, and they let me back in the car. I could see them exchanging glances and little smirks as we returned to the office.

EASY MONEY

My father, Reg. #10851, Joseph Thomas Parsons, loved to tell this story. He and a constable named Mattie were rookies together in East Central Saskatchewan in the early '30s. The Sons of Freedom, a Doukhobor sect led by Peter Verigin, were protesting what they considered persecution by the Canadian government, which was forcing Doukhobor children to attend regular schools against their parents' wishes. The Sons of Freedom were burning their homes and staging nude protests throughout that part of Saskatchewan. As the preserver of public tranquility, the RCMP was called upon to intercept and halt these demonstrations.

My father and Mattie had been detailed with several other RCMP members to interrupt a nude protest, arrest the participants and generally stifle the Sons of Freedom followers in their mission to create a disturbance. A large truck had been commandeered to haul the protesters away. The RCMP waded into the wall of flesh to make their arrests. It was commented later during debriefing that taking hold of an unclothed human being is a distinct challenge because of the complete lack of handles. The task was made even more difficult by the unwillingness of the arrestees to cooperate.

My father had encountered a naked 250-pound woman and, in the absence of a matron, used his resourcefulness to "take hold" and wrestle her up onto the bed of the truck. He was struggling mightily and happened to glance over at Mattie, who at that moment had his shoulder nestled against the winsome buttocks of a slim 18-year-old nude female protester. My father was obviously expending every ounce of energy, sweating profusely in an effort to hoist his charge onto the truck. Mattie looked over at him, winked and remarked, "Geez, Joe, and to think they're paying us 75 cents a day for this!"

I promptly and indignantly told my dad what had happened. He asked me what I had done to deserve it. When I explained, he told me it was a lucky thing they had returned to pick me up from the highway, because some wouldn't have. Somewhere in the exchange, I learned a lesson about humility and being accountable for my own actions.

My parents were happy in Yorkton, and when my father was offered a provincial magistrate position, he decided to retire from the RCMP. However, he changed his mind when he was also offered his commission in the Force. He was transferred to Regina where all sub inspectors received officer training. This consisted of instruction on sword handling, saluting techniques and the proper wearing of an officer's uniform, as well as studying the officer's handbook. (Today, the training has evolved into the Officer's Familiarization Course, whose curriculum is much more contemporary in nature and includes almost no etiquette or decorum instruction but instead addresses the structure of the Force, the composition and functioning of policy centres and managerial decision making.) There was a large and opulent officer's mess, and we lived in an officer's home on the parade square of the training division. I suspect much of my father's training took place in the mess. Being an officer at that time was a very exclusive club, and we were the ideal young family who looked like we had stepped right out of a Norman Rockwell painting.

In 1953, my father was transferred to Victoria as the division staffing officer for the province. It was a very challenging period for him, as the Force had recently taken over policing in the province from the BC Provincial Police. Many provincial policemen had transferred into the RCMP and had much to learn about the organization. My father spent most of his time travelling to various detachments throughout the province.

Dad had always been my hero, and his influence on me was profound, but by this time I was a teenager. Elvis Presley loomed large in my life and was the cause of serious family disruption. Our first real fight was during Elvis's first *Ed Sullivan Show* appearance, which we were watching on our first TV. Shocked by the depravity of Elvis's gyrating pelvis, my father leapt up and turned the TV off to shelter us from this beast. I immediately turned the TV back on. The battle that ensued endured well into my late teenage years. My hair got longer as my father's got shorter.

The culminating events in my teenage relationship with my father took place after his transfer to Whitehorse, Yukon, where he was the officer commanding. I became a full-time musician and party boy, playing in the Northernairs dance band in Whitehorse. My father and I barely spoke for at least two years. Through this transition I had lost most of my regard for anyone over 20, including my parents. However, when I emerged from adolescence, my love for the RCMP was intact, and I resumed my plan to join the Force.

I left the family home when I was 16. My parents transferred to Ottawa, where my father became commanding officer of G Division, a jurisdiction that encompassed the entire north but had its headquarters in the capital. He completed his career as senior personnel officer for the RCMP and retired in 1965. Although our later relationship was warm, it was never quite as adoring as it had been during my early years. He was a wonderful human being with a great zest for life and laughter and a huge personality. Whenever he was in a room, there would always be people gathered around him. That is how I will always remember him.

CHAPTER 2

STAND STILL, LOOK TO YOUR FRONT

As a boy, I attended the Roy Rogers Finishing School almost from the time I could walk. Classes were every Saturday afternoon at the York Theatre in Yorkton, a dusty prairie town. Along with my father, Roy was one of my earliest heroes. He taught me how to shoot straight, ride like the wind and always be on the right side of the law. He showed me it was possible to wipe out an entire nest of outlaws single-handed without even getting dirt on your fringed cowboy shirt. He taught me the difference between good and evil, and to always be kind to your horse.

When I was 18, I applied to join the RCMP. You had to be a male Canadian citizen, at least five feet eight inches tall, between 18 and 30 years of age, have a minimum education level of grade 10 and possess a valid driver's licence. I met all the basic qualifications except for the minimum height. Recruiters decreed I failed to measure up, dashing my hopes of following in my father's footsteps. Because I had played the trumpet since I was 10, my second option was to join a military band, so I elected to join the Canadian Army. Canada maintained a dozen military bands across the nation, one of which was based in Calgary. I successfully auditioned and became part of the trumpet section of the Lord Strathcona's Horse Regimental Band as a full-time professional.

Yet I hadn't totally abandoned my dream of joining the RCMP. The regiment also had a cavalry tradition and maintained a stable, where members could board their own horses for a nominal fee. Taking advantage of this, I purchased a young quarter horse, broke her to saddle and rode extensively during this period. Three years later, while visiting my parents, I discovered I had grown slightly, perhaps due to my long hours in the saddle. I was now officially tall enough to join the RCMP. I reactivated my application, had a fingerprint check and personal interview and was eventually presented with an offer of engagement, contingent upon resignation from the Canadian Armed Forces.

I returned to Calgary, obtained my honorable discharge from the army and was authorized to continue my indoctrination into the RCMP. My final hurdles were a complete medical checkup and a Minnesota Multiphasic Personality Inventory (MMPI) test, which was then the gold-standard test to detect personality disorders. After successfully proving my physical and psychological fitness, I was ordered to report to what was known then as Depot Division in Regina. On July 3, 1961, I became a member of "A" Troop. Assembled in Dormitory 3B was a motley, anxious group of 32 young men from across Canada, all apprehensive about our impending adventure.

Nine members of our group were francophone, several unable to speak English. Constable Rea, our troop leader and a recently graduated recruit, introduced himself as our supervisor. He openly expressed a dislike of francophones, decreeing at the outset that not one word of French be uttered. If a French recruit had the temerity to speak in his native tongue, fellow recruits were to discipline him in tried-and-true RCMP tradition—cold showers or blackballing (which consisted of restraining the victim and applying liberal amounts of black shoe polish to his testicles). Discriminating against candidates from Quebec was considered justifiable, as it accelerated their integration into the predominant English culture. Francophone candidates who managed to complete training were possessed of an iron resolve. I found it unimaginable that one could withstand the trauma of basic recruit training while not comprehending the commands. It was amazing, yet somehow understandable, how quickly they grasped basic profane English. Successful French-speaking recruits routinely returned to Quebec following training, their sole memories of English-speaking Canada being the agonizing months they spent at Depot. No doubt the degrading treatment they suffered as recruits caused residual resentment toward English Canada and the rest of the nation for the duration of their service. As they gained seniority and rose in the ranks, ill feelings lingered, echoing the antipathy felt by many in La Belle Province toward the rest of Canada.

On the first morning of training we were issued a basic uniform of green fatigues. We were now identifiable as rabble, which made us fair game for instructors and senior recruits alike. Constantly hounded, yelled at and scourged, we reeled from place to place for the first week. Forbidden to march, we moved about as a frenetic amoeba, always on the double. Thankfully, new troops arrived each week to begin their training, which lessened some of the pressure on us. During those first two weeks an astounding amount of kit and clothing was issued to each man. To neophyte policemen, the regalia and equipment were mysterious and alluring.

Rank, seniority and structure were the mortar that held together the bricks of the Academy. The senior troops felt they had as much authority and influence over our miserable lives as the instructors. The senior squads resided in a separate building connected to our 32-bed dormitory by a steam-heating tunnel. One evening, as we sat cloistered in our dorm, we heard a strange rumbling sound. Suddenly, the doors exploded open and we were invaded by two troops of seniors. We stood little chance, as they outnumbered us two to one. They upended our beds scattered our kit and hauled many of us off to the showers. The raid was over in minutes, the horde disappearing as quickly as it had arrived. These dorm invasions occurred sporadically during our time in

Depot. Occasionally there were injuries and damage, but nothing was ever reported. From time to time, directives were issued from the upper echelon describing the raids as unacceptable, yet little was ever done officially to stop them. Hazing was part of the training experience, but a sad reflection of man's innate cruelty to man.

Our first physical training (PT) session consisted of a five-mile run, clearly meant to cull the weakest. Instructors ran with us, spelling each other off as they tired so they could keep up a blistering pace. Several of our group fell by the wayside, collapsing from exhaustion. Following the run, we were reassembled only to be berated and insulted by the instructors. According to the physical training staff, the likelihood of any of us surviving Depot was faint. For $150 a recruit could buy his way out of training, and they encouraged us to do this immediately. Apparently, the organization was very difficult to enter but quite simple to exit. Much discussion took place that evening, with some of my discouraged troop-mates considering their options.

To some recruits, the physical segment of RCMP training was cruel, even sadistic. There is no question it was rigorous and tough, typifying the stress model used by police and military organizations during that era. Instructors sincerely believed the harsh treatment they inflicted would prepare their charges for the stresses and strains of police work. As law-enforcement training evolved, a more humane but equally demanding regimen was adopted. However, back in the early 1960s, a typical session involved the troop working to a fever pitch through running and calisthenics. In varying states of exhaustion, recruits were forced to roll on the gym floor until they became nauseous. Many would lie in their own vomit, too winded and demoralized to move. These sessions were commonly referred to as torture periods.

Boxing and police-hold instruction presented additional opportunities to test individual courage. The troop members were arranged in a circle around a mat, and two individuals were selected to don boxing gloves and pummel each another. Very little actual instruction took place, even though several of the instructors were experienced boxers. If a recruit possessed boxing training or talent, he would be chosen to spar with an instructor. The combination of the recruit's hesitancy to strike his mentor and the instructor's skills usually resulted in a one-sided affair. Our instruction in effective police holds followed a similar pattern. Any PT session could quickly regress into a torture period if the instructors detected any kind of infraction, real or imagined. Over time, we also received formalized training in gymnastics.

The swimming instructors held their own enlightened approach to training. Even those of us with experience in the water learned to dread these draconian sessions. The swimming program began at the edge of the pool, where we learned accepted RCMP movements. A particularly sadistic sergeant we secretly referred to as "Captain Chlorine" presided over the mayhem. We lay spread-eagled on our stomachs while instructors with bamboo canes "guided" us through the drill. Any deviation from the accepted method was corrected with sharp strikes on the legs and feet. When it was time to move into the pool, non-swimmers were forced to jump off the high board into the deep end. When it looked like they were about to drown, they were pulled from the pool with the assistance of long poles. At the end of the swimming course, the more competent members of the troop were tested for the Red Cross award of merit. In one segment of the test, the instructor posed as a drowning swimmer. When the recruit approached the panic-stricken "victim," he attempted to place the victim in a towing position. If the recruit did not perform exactly as taught, the instructor would grab him in a death grip and take him to the bottom of the pool. Release only occurred when the rescuer was on the brink of panic himself.

Within a month, the pressures of training began to take their toll, and several of the troop decided to leave. By the sixth week, nine members had resigned. It occurred to our instructors that they might be able to completely eradicate "A" Troop—now reduced to 23 members—if they maintained the intensity. They redoubled their efforts to eliminate those of us who remained. In their zeal to decimate our numbers, the physical training staff identified three of us as being under the magic minimum height of five foot eight. Even though we were coping with the challenges being thrown our way, we were measured once, twice and three times. Still not satisfied, they called in experts from the provincial weights and measures ministry. The process went on for several weeks and was thoroughly demoralizing. Finally we appeared before the division medical officer. I recall sitting in his office when he concluded his interview by asking me if I wished to continue my training. My response was resoundingly positive. He finally put an end to our misery by certifying in each of our files that we met the minimum-height requirement.

The arbitrary minimum-height rules introduced us to discrimination that exists in a general way in many societies but is particularly rampant in a military setting. In the RCMP the mean height is somewhere between five foot ten and six foot two, and those who fell on either side of this "ideal" height range were constantly reminded of it. Members on the tall end of the scale also suffered constant, repetitive and often tasteless comments about their seeming affliction. In calling out members who were above or below the mean height, the training staff communicated the God-given right of all to identify physical aberrations. Throughout my years on the Force, I was subjected to comments regarding my height (though civilians have rarely commented on it). Usually it was good-natured ribbing, but sometimes there were overtones of cruelty and sarcasm. It is a strange and somewhat motivating cross to bear. Singled out for what some labelled a physical deficit, I was even more determined to perform to the best of my ability. Even during gatherings of retired RCMP veterans, there are invariably comments about one's extra height or lack thereof.

To ensure the survival of our small squad, bonds developed and vows were made. As we came to know each other better, individual personalities emerged and added to the tapestry of the troop. Parker was our right marker, the one who formed us up for parade, called the roll and generally responded on our behalf to commands. Markers were selected for their military bearing and appearance in uniform. We learned that these physical attributes were used to identify leaders, though it was clear even during basic training that an impeccable appearance did not always indicate an effective leader. Our right marker was a classic example. Parker was a true peacock, always looking the part and projecting a noble presence, but in reality he was a scoundrel in sheep's clothing, constantly looking for ways to create havoc and disarray. He was responsible for a number of incidents that shone a negative light upon us. During our orientation to the small arms range, the instructor demonstrated his prowess with a .38 special revolver. After firing several rounds at the target, he realized none of the rounds had even hit the paper upon which the target was mounted. Puzzled, he walked down the range, only to find his rounds had not even made it to the target and were lying on the floor. He checked the box of shells from which he had loaded the weapon and discovered that all the bullets in the box had been tampered with. Someone had removed the lead and emptied out some of the powder. Enraged, he demanded to know who was responsible. No one admitted to the prank, so the entire troop was confined to barracks. After several days, Parker confessed. He was further punished for his stunt, but the troop carried the stigma of his actions. His actual career in the force was very brief, as he fell into several serious disciplinary jams related to finances and was eventually dismissed.

Also in our midst was a young Charney Biln, the first Sikh ever to join the Force. His first posting would be in Drumheller, Alberta, where he was immediately accepted and respected by the community. Tragically, Charney and his new wife lost their lives in a traffic accident just three years into his service. Francois Dubois, one of our prevailing French-Canadian candidates, was so physically attractive that women would actually stalk him when he walked the streets of Regina. Young and inexperienced, Francois was completely mystified by the strange spell he cast over the opposite sex. He too would die in a traffic accident early in his service.

Dick Havers, the eldest of our group, was a 25-year-old who had left the Air Force to join the RCMP. His air of superiority thrust him into almost daily conflict with instructors. Dave Tough, a young man from the Maritimes, was so physically awkward he could not swing his arms and march at the same time. Tough suffered unmercifully at the hands of PT instructors. His common sense and mature philosophy were in direct contrast to his deficient coordination, though. He persevered through the agony of training to become one of the most successful of our number in his police career. Another troop-mate, R.R. Bouck, went to British Columbia where he had a distinguished career in detachment policing, winning two commissioner's commendations for bravery. Terry David Mulligan, one of the youngest in the troop, briefly served in Alberta, where he discovered his talents lay in the field of broadcasting. He left the Force after three short years and went on to be a radio and television personality in the Vancouver area. Don Gamble, a farm boy from Gull Lake, Saskatchewan, became one of Canada's foremost handwriting experts while serving with the RCMP Crime Detection Laboratory. There were clowns and cut-ups, young men of serious mien, naïve farm boys and those who really had no idea why they were there. It was amazing to witness the melding of divergent personalities into a single cohesive unit.

After a few short weeks, Sergeant Major MacRae, perhaps the most highly visible symbol of power and authority in the training division, met with us in a classroom. He informed us that our diminished number was creating logistical problems since the curriculum was predicated on 32-man units. He was considering dissolving the troop and distributing its individuals to incoming squads. We pleaded with him to allow the troop to remain intact, assuring him we would cope with the challenges. He reluctantly agreed, granting us a trial period.

FOR INSPECTION

One of the more impressive movements performed by RCMP recruits during their dismounted cavalry drills is a movement called "For Inspection, Draw Revolvers." The 32-person troop lines up in two rows of 16. The right marker is situated at the extreme right front and choreographs the action with head movements.

On a sunny July day, our troop was preparing for our drill graduation. Being the senior troop, we were at the front of the daily noon parade. This parade is a time-honoured tradition. It takes place on the main square in the training division and launches the recruit troops to their afternoon classes. Knowing that we were going to be demonstrating the "For Inspection" movement, we anxiously awaited the order from the sergeant major, which came suddenly.

Our right marker took three smart paces to the front and snapped an "eyes left," his every move scrutinized by his troop-mates, acting in unison and on cue. When the right marker nodded his head slightly, we simultaneously moved our right hands and slapped our revolver holsters. Another nod and the holster flap was undone, right hand on the weapon. On the order from the sergeant major, revolvers were drawn and held with the elbow bent at a precise 45 degree angle, ready for inspection. As the weapons moved like lightning to this position, the right marker snapped his head to the front and took three paces back to be in line with the troop. Much to the his horror, when he moved his head to the front, he saw a condom hanging from the barrel of his revolver, placed there in advance by some prankster. Was there a lesson to be learned here concerning the securing of one's personal revolver at all times?

Our right marker was outraged! Was this an indictable offence? Would his all-too-brief career be terminated because of a condom? He was frozen in terror, unable to react. As the sergeant major approached, the right marker uttered a silent prayer to assist him in his departure from this world. The sergeant major faced him with a look of total scorn and disgust. Gingerly, he lifted the condom from the barrel of the gun with his drill baton, sauntered over to the parade square curb and relegated the offending item to the tarmac.

The parade continued to its conclusion. The throngs of spectators gathered to view the parade seemed to have missed the debacle. Following the parade, the "usual suspects" were intensely interrogated. The code of silence was invoked and no leads surfaced to identify the culprit. Life went on. Our right marker likely remained celibate for the remainder of his days.

As a troop, we set objectives to match the other troops and exceed their performance if possible. In the ensuing weeks, we were able to withstand everything the instructors threw our way and managed to settle into a routine. Our small troop coped with all the duties of a larger squad and earned a measure of unique regard from the training staff.

The foot drill instructors rated high on our fear quotient. They seemed to be rewarded within the RCMP hierarchy for their haughtiness and arrogance. Tall, slim and prepossessing in their gleaming leather and shining brass, they strutted about the complex, swinging their distinctive batons. Their raison d'etre was to discover anything that might deviate from a perfect recruit turnout. Five o' clock shadows, scuffed boots, undone buttons or specks of lint were all small victories to be discovered by these stentorian-voiced nitpickers. Political correctness was unheard of back then, and ethnicity, skin colour or unusual names were all sources of great interest and delight. One unfortunate recruit with African genes and a French name was immediately christened "Coon Frog" and addressed by that name for the duration of his stay in the training division. French names were ridiculed and bastardized, as were Slavic and Italian names.

RCMP foot drill formations are based on mounted cavalry drills, where troops moved in eight-person sections. They are extremely precise, requiring hours of practice. We were a cavalry regiment but carried rifles during drills, which made the movements more complex. Complete and utter stillness was expected until an order to enact a specific movement was issued. Miscues were not tolerated and miscreants were sentenced to 25 push-ups, to be completed immediately while attired in boots and breeches. At the whim of the instructor, the troop would be commanded to break into double-time movement for the duration of the drill hour. By the time it ended, our tunics and high brown boots were stained with white sweat marks.

One shimmering prairie July day, the commanding officer was escorting a group of clergy about the grounds. When they entered the beautiful regimental chapel, they discovered three recruits in full dress kneeling at the altar. When asked about their seeming devoutness, they explained their drill instructor had found them so despicable on the drill square that they were sent to the chapel to pray for forgiveness. Drill instructors were routinely hated at the outset of training, but then, strangely, they would emerge to become the best loved of all instructors. Many of us attributed this strange outcome to Stockholm syndrome.

In our first two months at Depot, we faced many tough challenges. Most of us had survived the initial hurdles put in our way, but a bigger barrier lay ahead. The recruit population typically regarded the riding stables with fear and awe, and we were about to learn why.

CHAPTER 3

RIDE, TROT!

"**P**arsons, your mother shoulda thrown you out and kept the afterbirth, you useless little man!" Those words uttered by my riding instructor remain with me to this day. In 1966, equitation training was withdrawn from the curriculum. The stables in Regina were closed and the horses moved to Rockcliffe, Ontario, which became the home of the RCMP Musical Ride. This decision transformed the Academy in Regina forever. Although many senior RCMP officers subscribed to Winston Churchill's oft-repeated phrase, "There is something about the outside of a horse that is good for the inside of a man," this change freed up 140 hours within the curriculum for more contemporary law-enforcement topics. But in 1961, the stables influenced the entire Depot experience, both positively and negatively.

After two months at Depot, we began our mounted training, which was in addition to academic subjects, practical training, typing classes, PT, swimming and foot drill. Our indoctrination into equitation presented another rite of passage, complete with unique and intense rituals and routines.

Some members of the troop had never been up close and personal with a horse. These magnificent animals were like spoiled children and took advantage of every opportunity to show recruits that they were the prima donnas of the paddock. We had to earn our spurs, so these essential tools were denied us for the first 60 hours of riding. The horses were aware of this and generally ignored us, even when we were astride them. The riding staff hounded us constantly to move our mounts along, but no amount of urging with knees and heels would work. We functioned with minimal responses from our steeds and maximum yelling and insults from the riding staff. After hours of recalcitrant horses and assaultive instructors, we were finally allowed to don our spurs. Each and every man looked forward with glee to the next riding session when we could force our will upon our stubborn mounts; however, when the distinctive jingle of spurs reached the horses' sensitive ears, they suddenly complied with every command. We would seldom have the opportunity to inflict our revenge. The few who tried quickly learned how challenging it was to control a horse's enthusiasm when it was even slightly goaded by a spur.

The riding stable staff was devoted solely to the horses, which were pampered, groomed, pedicured and fed as though they were sacred beings. RCMP mounts had evolved from providing everyday transportation during the Force's early years to serving in ceremonial occasions after the advent of the automobile. These changing needs called for a different type of horse, and a breeding program was started in 1939. In 1943, the program became more sophisticated as Clydesdales, Percherons, Hanoverians and Trakehners were bred with thoroughbreds to produce a heavier-boned, well-mannered, hardy horse. The RCMP mount transformed into the majestic black animal now seen in the musical ride, approximately 16 hands in height, weighing between 1,200 and 1,300 pounds.

The 60 horses in the Depot stables were all offspring of the breeding program, though some exceptions in colour, weight and height were forgiven for training purposes. These haughty creatures were the stars of the show, and they were acutely aware of it. Much like people, they possessed distinctive personalities, some engaging, some wary, some cranky and some downright vicious. When the list was posted on the day previous to a ride, we were keen to find out which horses we had been assigned to. If you were unfortunate enough to draw Waco, a red-haired biter, you knew she would put a welt on you before the day was out. Those assigned Wasp and Rogue were assured a relatively easy ride, as both reflected their docile Clydesdale heritage. Still, they presented their own challenges; they were large in girth and stood 18 hands high, making a graceful mount almost impossible. Imp and Epic were small, dainty, responsive animals that were a pleasure to ride. Gorse the horse was slow-witted and slow-moving.

One of the most interesting characters in the entire stable was a gelding named Rob Roy. He was a beautiful animal, and it was easy to see why he used to be a stud. After being replaced by two younger stallions, he was gelded and put into the riding pool. He developed a most interesting, albeit annoying habit that may have illustrated his disgust at losing his stallion status. When lined up for any kind of inspection, Rob Roy let his very sizable tongue hang out of his mouth, protruding some six to eight inches. Instructors delighted in taunting new riders who were unaware of the unusual habit. A recruit who had drawn Rob Roy would stand at attention beside his mount, awaiting inspection. An instructor would bellow at the neophyte, commanding him to get his mount's tongue back into its mouth. The terrified recruit would desperately attempt to reinstall Rob Roy's tongue, to no avail. He would be upbraided for having no control over the horse, with additional observations on the unlikelihood of him ever becoming a policeman.

Our riding instructor was Corporal Landers, a lithe young man born to the saddle and barely older than his charges. Our first mounted foray took us onto the bald prairie in troop formation. After an hour on the trail, we halted for a break and enjoyed an informal chat. Terry Mulligan, who hailed from mountainous British Columbia, gestured gleefully to a small mound where the revolver range was located. He jokingly asked the corporal if it was the largest mountain in Saskatchewan. Corporal Landers, who was a Saskatchewan native, glared at Mulligan, commanding him to dismount. Dressing him down as a smart ass, he ordered him to start running. Mulligan immediately obeyed, loping across the prairie. The corporal spurred his horse, Laura, into action. Ears laid back and teeth bared, she pursued the recruit, running him to the ground. Landers commanded Mulligan to get up and run, then repeated the process. This continued for the duration of the return trip to the stables, by which time Constable Mulligan was a mass of torn clothing and cuts. It became glaringly obvious that flippancy with a riding instructor invited disaster. We were beginning to understand that the objective of equitation was not to transform us into accomplished horsemen, but to further test our mettle. The riding program was an opportunity to assess the courage of individual recruits by placing them in sometimes terrifying situations, limited only by the instructor's imagination.

Recruits were responsible for all menial daily stable duties. Each morning, selected troops would appear at reveille to scour stalls, followed by feeding and grooming. Many of the horses made sport with recruits, kicking and biting them. The more timid members were sent into box stalls to groom the stallions. Unfettered, the powerful beasts challenged anyone who entered, baring their teeth and striking out with their hooves. It was a daunting experience for someone who was city-bred and had never encountered such an intimidating animal. During morning stable duty, the horses were led to water troughs located at the centre of the barns. Recruits were detailed two horses each, leading them by the halter. Enjoying their bit of freedom, the horses took the opportunity to kick and bite the recruits and each other. Trying to maintain control of two horses while they watered and kibitzed was a daunting challenge. The instructors waited until the horses were lined up to drink, then fired a rifle containing a blank cartridge, startling the horses and creating additional havoc. The unfortunate recruits caught in the melee were tossed to and fro as they clung to the animals, occasionally incurring injuries.

During one afternoon session, the troop was riding in single-file formation in the indoor riding ménage. Several instructors sat on their horses in the centre. Suddenly, Corporal Landers spurred his horse into action, hurtling straight for me with Laura's ears back and teeth bared. My horse and I were almost bowled over when they collided with us. As he hurled several obscenities my way, it was clear that Landers had just learned I was the son of a commissioned officer. Landers assured me that my life would be a misery henceforth, and he fulfilled that promise for the rest of our time in the stables.

As equitation training progressed, we began to grasp rudimentary musical ride movements. The troop would move four abreast, trotting and cantering under the tutelage of the instructor. The constant, repetitive commands from those days will resonate in my memory forever: "Ride, trot!" "Get your lower legs back!" "You there on Rob Roy, take the rear of the ride!" "Four feet, nose to croup!" One curious city-bred pupil innocently asked an instructor what a "croup" was. The instructor escorted him over to the hindquarters of a mare standing in her stall. He lifted the horse's tail and urged the young member to peer closely. When the recruit got into position, the instructor placed his hand at the back of his student's head and rammed his face into the rear portion of the horse. "That, young constable, is a croup," explained the corporal.

Frequently, the horses became spirited at the canter, bucking and making it difficult to hold one's seat. Tex Burris, a tough, wiry young man from Ontario, tried to control his steed while it bucked and sidestepped. As the troop moved at the canter, Burris lost his balance, tumbling over the flanks of the horse. As he went down, the horse kicked, striking him. The ride was immediately halted. Unable to stand, Burris tried to pull himself along with his arms. Corporal Landers, astride his horse, stood over Burris, commanding him to stand. When it became obvious Burris was injured, the corporal delegated two of the troop to "remove the rabble from the riding school." More concerned about the horse than the recruit, he then called for someone to examine it for injuries. Later, Burris was found to have a broken pelvis.

In the jargon of recruits, a "perfect day" consisted of PT, foot drill and swimming in the first half of the training day, followed by equitation for the latter half. These activities were physically demanding, and we had to go through hours of kit preparation before we rode. Prior to a morning or afternoon ride, recruits were expected to attend the stables and scour their tack. Our work was closely inspected at the start of the class. Any recruit whose saddle and bridle were not properly presented would be paraded to the sergeant major and punished with extra duties in the form of guard mount or fatigue duty, which encompassed all hard labour such as rubbing, cleaning, mopping and polishing.

As our training continued, a Saskatchewan winter descended. Daily temperatures in December were often lower than 30 below. On weekends, two troops were assigned to the stables for a morning exercise ride. Prior to going out into the cracking cold, the horses were fed hot bran. The aroma of breakfast cooking caused the horses to nicker and impatiently stomp their hooves. Once the horses had eaten, the recruits saddled up, put on the famous RCMP buffalo coat to fend off the cold and ventured out. The horses, having been confined to the stables overnight and now filled with hot bran, were restless, mischievous and strangely eager to leave their warm home. As the mounted troop exited, and the horses hit the cold air, a chemical reaction seemed to occur. One of the horses would release a gigantic fart, bucking and kicking as he expended his gas. This signalled to the others to do likewise, and chaos would reign. On one occasion, before control was regained, furry mounds of buffalo fur, breeches and spurs were randomly distributed in the snow adjacent to the horse barn. To a man, the troop had been involuntarily dismounted. The instructors were greatly entertained by the fiasco and roared at the riders to recapture their horses and remount.

Over and above our equitation duties, four members of our troop had joined the training division's drum and bugle corps. Volunteers came from various troops, and the band would play simple marches during the traditional one o'clock parade following the lunch hour. The only troops excused from the parade were those assigned to afternoon equitation. Realizing the band was the darling of Sergeant Major MacRae, and knowing he was watching us carefully, we had volunteered for his band to convey our enthusiasm and troop spirit. This display of initiative worked in our favour until we missed our afternoon ride because we were performing with the bugle band on the parade square. As the troop lined up for inspection prior to the ride, Corporal Landers noticed it was conspicuously reduced in number. He demanded to know where the missing four members were. When he learned we were on the square playing in the bugle band, he waited for our appearance, some 30 minutes late. Landers promptly rechristened us with names to reflect our musical endeavours: Beethoven, Mozart, Ravel and Strauss. As a penalty for our late appearance at the riding stables, we received extra attention during the equitation session. Following the harangue by the riding instructors, the four of us decided not to arrive late for another equitation class. When equitation was scheduled for the troop, we were present for riding inspection.

Later that day we were summoned to the office of the sergeant major, who demanded to know why we were absent from the band. After our explanation, he made it absolutely clear what would happen to us if we again failed to appear with the bugle band. When we asked him how we should cope with our riding instructor, he said to leave that to him. We could only imagine what transpired between the riding staff and the sergeant major, but no words were spoken when we appeared late for our next equitation class. However, we were still called by our musical names while in the stable and were appropriately persecuted in small ways for the remainder of our riding days. We were assigned difficult horses, given the less palatable jobs in the stables and frequently assigned the intimidating task of grooming the stallions, in addition to many other tasks that would make our lives more difficult.

My musical talents would further complicate my quest for a law-enforcement career. At the halfway point of our training, I was summoned to the personnel office and asked if I had any interest in joining the RCMP band in Ottawa. I respectfully declined, telling the interviewer I wished to work as a policeman. Several weeks later, they once again contacted me, this time *informing* me that I was to go to Ottawa at the conclusion of training to join the band. At the time, the RCMP band was only a part-time organization with musicians holding down administrative jobs and playing as and when required. Extremely agitated and disappointed, I explained that prior to joining the RCMP I had been a member of one of the premier regimental bands in North America. I said that if they assigned me to the RCMP band, I would return to the regimental army band. No doubt my response caused some irritation, but I heard nothing more about this and was allowed to continue on my path to a law-enforcement career.

LIFE SAVER? I THINK NOT! _____

His name was Willie George. Willie was one of two "stallions in waiting" in the RCMP stables. He was as black as his heart and stood 17 hands high; his eyes burned with hatred. He resided in a box stall, and when there was a mare in heat nearby he created unimaginable havoc. He would bang his stall constantly, and his snorts and screams would fill the entire barn. Recruits ceased to be assigned to groom him as he had injured so many of them. Only two of the most experienced riding instructors would saddle and ride him.

Having owned a horse prior to joining the Force, I fancied myself something of a "horse whisperer." I discovered that Willie had a weakness for Wint O Green Life Savers, so I would stop by his stall from time to time and give him this treat. As time wore on, I noticed he would look for me. He seemed almost civil as I fed him the Life Savers, and my confidencein dealing with him was growing, as was the admiration from my troopmates. I eventually gathered the courage to open his door and feed him the Life Savers face to face. Things were going quite well for Willie and me, and my fame as a horse handler was spreading.

Occasionally, recruits were assigned stable orderly duties. This meant that two of us would be in the stables all night, cleaning gutters and feeding and watering the horses. On this particular evening the horses had just received their nightly ration of oats. This was obviously the highlight of the horses' daily routine, and their anticipation was palpable as the oats were doled out. Willie George had just been given his share and was munching contentedly. I opened his door and approached him with my stash of Life Savers. We shared a bond now. But when I held out my hand, he nudged it away. I must have totally forgotten whom I was dealing with. I approached him again with the Life Savers. I cannot recall precisely what happened next, but suddenly I felt a searing pain in my upper arm. Then I flew through the air and smashed against the stall, crumpling in the corner. I looked up at four long black legs and the stallion's head as he quietly munched his oats, then I quietly crawled out of the stall. Willie George had bitten through my pea jacket, inner jacket and shirt and thrown me across the box stall. Our relationship was over, as was my brief career as a tamer of stallions, and I was left with feelings of abject humility. I never bought Wint O Green Life Savers again.

As the troop moved through the equitation program, we developed some semblance of rapport with our instructor. Christmas was approaching, and we asked Corporal Landers if we could buy him a holiday drink. Amazingly, he invited the entire troop to his home one Saturday afternoon. His wife was absent when a large number of us arrived there, liberally supplied with bottles of Christmas cheer. As the afternoon went on, several of the revellers became inebriated. Eric Crampton developed an infatuation with the corporal, depositing his six-foot-three-inch, 230-pound body in his lap, hugging him enthusiastically. No amount of coaxing from the victim or troop members would sway him from his drunken fondness. Another guest fell over the large ornate Christmas tree, knocking it down. Still another staggered down the basement steps, spilling a drink and putting a dent in the washing machine. By the time the troop departed, we knew we had overstayed our welcome.

Even though several troop members immediately returned to the scene of the crime to clean up and make things right, it was glaringly evident that our rapport with Corporal Landers was forever sullied. When "A" Troop returned to the riding academy to continue our equitation training, we realized we would be paying for our indiscretions. For the remaining 50 hours of our riding classes, we were seldom astride our steeds. Instead, we performed all of the required formations on foot while leading the horses. At the conclusion of our riding pass out, Corporal Landers, in the company of the entire riding staff, informed us we were the worst troop to ever pass through Depot. We were told to exit the stables and never come back.

We returned to the rest of our training curriculum with enthusiasm, thankful that equitation was behind us. For many of us, any love and admiration we held for horses would be forever tainted as a result of our RCMP training experience.

—— THE LAST POST ——

The following poem was written by Constable J.K. Crosby (January 19, 1939–March 25, 2009), a member of RCMP "A" Troop, 1958, at "Depot" Division, Regina, Saskatchewan. "A" Troop gathered for a reunion in 1994, where Ken Crosby presented these memories of equitation training.

On quiet days a sudden flash, a scent,
A sound, or something else to stir the other time
A shout, a distant roll of drums
A marching tune or bugle on the wind
Can summon up the pride of what has been
The memories report for watch again

A clopping horse's hoof re-echoing on the pavement
Although there be no horse
The ammonia blast of the overnight void
Although there be no stalls
The warmth beneath the curry comb and brush
The warm neck to lay a head on
The gruffness that hid the real affection

The strength, the firmness of shoulder and haunch,
The might, the fright, her of me, and me of her.
A fright to overcome with persistence and love.
The warmness of the horse's teary eye
Its nodding head approving the affection given
Responding with a recognition that
Although ridden by others, the horse was truly yours.
Their names flash by from time to time
My "Gypsy", a "Rebel", "Dawn" and "Gail"
A "Rogue" that really wasn't and a "Faux Pas" that was

I remember "Newton" biting Sam Strang's thumb
Strang the Roughrider, Harry Armstrong, Ralph Cave,
Jesse Jessiman
They're still forming troops in my memory
and making sure that we used the saddle soap
On our supple fragrant tack.
Still shouting "Ride, prepare to mount"
As I hear again the leathery grunting squeak of the stirrups
And saddles along the assembled line of exhaling horses.

By sections and half sections through weather's best and worst
Enough cold to freeze a breath and steam and ice a horse
Enough warmth to quickly sweat and bring froth to a horse's coat
I remember the scent of the horse's sweat
Its warmth and its wetness
Its feeling on my cheek as I hugged the horse's neck

Its smell on my clothing
Its splash between my fingers as I "Made Much" to my horse.

I remember jumps, my grunts, the horse's grunts, the awkward landings,
the surprise I was still mounted
And suicide lane and the order "quit reins, quit stirrups"
Tipping a forage cap was never so funny
As when doffed by a rider with weak knees
A rider with weak knees shouting "Good morning Corporaaal"

I remember "Roman Riding" and "field days"
That were more of a day-off than "General Equitation"
I remember a big inflated ball that stood as high as a horse's withers
Except for "Gaul" of course, who stood seventeen hands
I remember the soft tilled soil of the Riding School
As opposed to the gumbo outside
That exacted such punishment to our ironed Strathcona boots
That were spit shined, be they Hart made or McDonnell.
I remember "the ride", I remember the precision
I remember the gaits, the canter figure of eight
The pleasure of having missed hitting anyone in the crossover.
I remember wondering how the music kept in time so well
with the "bump trot"
And in the Riding School, there came those fleeting fantasies
of those great cavalries that had gone before
From the Cossacks on the steppes through to the Strathcona Horse
From the Charge of the Light Brigade to the United States Seventh
From the Great March from Dufferin of the Northwest Mounted.

They were all united somehow in one force, in one panorama,
One bonded unison.
Men and horses operating across time with pride and precision,
The pride and precision of Cavalrymen
The brotherhood of the saddle who had to "earn their spurs",

They rise to ride again, though fleetingly,
As "A" Troop '58 answers its last muster.
Now silvered and weathered and slower than those days of youth
As mounted troopers
We still maintain that pride of a great tradition
Of being that tradition's last
We store up scents and sounds and wispy scenes
That rise to flood our thoughts from time to time
That none now make and few have leave to claim.

We horsemen, we brothers, we the eternally locked unit of man
and mount
Can look upon the path we made to see that it made us
And sometimes see the glory that it was,
Its moments, its comrades, its mounts, all last a lifetime
And all these things still summon to our call
From that branded special corner of our Cavalry hearts.

The academic side of the curriculum continued to be extremely demanding. The remaining months of training were filled with hours of criminal law, federal statutes, report writing, forensic identification, memory and observation, practical training and firearms training. Typing, perhaps the single most important physical skill in police work, was taught in a concentrated fashion that produced competent typists within a few short hours. To compel practice and familiarity, recruits typed pages upon pages of criminal statutes after each law class.

The firing ranges were perhaps the only areas of training devoid of sarcasm and sadism. The emphasis was on safety and becoming proficient handlers of firearms. Many hours were devoted to the mechanics, care and maintenance of our weapons before we were allowed to actually fire them. Ammunition was carefully controlled and inventoried, and students had to empty their pockets at the end of each session. Although this critical aspect of recruit training was conducted with great professionalism, it was an era preceding modern workplace health regulations. Thousands of young men left training with irreparable hearing damage from using firearms without ear protection. Those few who dared to mention discomfort due to the constant explosions were told to place expended brass cartridges in their ears. Instead of deadening the sound, the cartridges actually amplified it.

Each day brought information overload, and we had to cram constantly for ongoing exams. Driver training and foot drill were also high-profile subjects. Our driver-training outings afforded us our first opportunity to be viewed by the public in our revered RCMP uniforms. Escorted into local cafés by our mentors, we would descend like a gaggle of geese, experiencing what all policemen fondly view as the cult of the coffee break. We ventured into rural areas surrounding the city to learn the basics of defensive and interceptive driving from an instructing corporal. All of our driver-training instructors were seasoned field personnel, happy to share their tales and anecdotes from the field. We hung on every word they uttered.

Although driver training was our first exposure to the public while in uniform, our shorn heads and formal manner made us readily identifiable even when we wore civilian clothes in downtown Regina during our off-duty hours. Almost since the RCMP began training recruits in Regina, there has been discernible polarization between local young men and RCMP trainees. It has ebbed and flowed through the years with the occasional eruption. Shortly prior to our arrival in the training division, several members of another troop attended one of the local dance clubs. They were confronted and outnumbered by a group of unruly youths. A scuffle broke out and several RCMP members were badly beaten, primarily because they were outnumbered. The perpetrators were well-known hoodlums who hung out regularly at a popular watering hole. The city police attended the melee, but no charges were laid due to identification issues. Being uncomfortable with possible negative publicity, RCMP management declined to take any further action.

The drill instructor of this particular troop was Sergeant Baldy Weathers, who was infamous for his fiery temper. When he learned of the incident, Sergeant Weathers decided to mete out some justice of his own. He gathered the entire troop and found them more than willing to become involved. The following weekend, armed with riding crops, the sergeant and his hit squad attended the establishment, sought out the troublemakers and soundly thrashed them. As the young men targeted were known bullies, even the locals endorsed the action. However, the RCMP powers that be were very unhappy with the spontaneous vigilante action and disciplined the sergeant and the recruits. They were charged in service court, where the participating recruits were fined and Sergeant Weathers was reduced in rank. In spite of this, he remained a member of the Force for many years, eventually regaining his stripes and enjoying legendary status for the remainder of his service.

FINALLY, AFTER ALMOST 10 months of an indescribable emotional and physical gauntlet, it was over. The remaining weeks were dedicated to our pass-out parade. We received our postings, and I learned I was to be stationed in Alberta. When graduation day finally arrived, the troop performed a drill and physical training display. A brief ceremony took place with family looking on, and we were on our way. RCMP basic training had been an odyssey unequalled in our young lives and would be remembered as an experience that few would want to relive, yet none would have missed. We were forever transformed and bound together by the blood, sweat and tears generated by those 10 traumatic months.

While most of us had gained confidence and maturity, some recruits left Depot Division with scars, both psychological and physical. RCMP candidates have always been rigidly screened, and most of those with unacceptable personality flaws or neurotic tendencies are eliminated. However, after being subjected to months of intense mental and physical rigours without the option of retaliating, it is safe to say that some pent-up emotions accompanied us as we departed. The need to lash out existed to varying degrees among recruits. In that era of little public scrutiny and police accountability, the combination of our punitive training experience and youthful exuberance sometimes exploded into very physical confrontations. Encountering an abusive, aggressive, drunken offender could be enough to turn a young policeman into an avenging angel. Sometimes a belligerent miscreant would suffer the consequences. It might even be surmised that a young policeman was subconsciously assuming the identity of a training instructor and the offender targeted was seen as the recruit.

As police training evolved and more was learned about human behaviour, it became clear the negative and punitive stress model employed for so many years could be improved upon. In the 1960s, the RCMP was still run like the NWMP in many ways, and our training was based on the cavalry-regiment tenets of the original 19th-century Force. Even though the curriculum was embellished with police-based subjects, the finished product was nothing more and nothing less than a well-trained soldier. We responded instantly to commands and learned to never question the directions of a superior. We were fodder for our first detachment commander, who had experienced an identical indoctrination. As young policemen, we hoped to be guided by commanders who could be emulated, but in most cases their management tools were forged by their own training and experience. Even if our commanders had the benefit of some in-service training, such courses focused on operational matters and investigational techniques rather than management skills. They devoted little time to motivating subordinates or encouraging career development. The system was tried and true and had worked for decades, but cracks were beginning to show even as we departed the training division to begin our careers.

CHAPTER 4

WELCOME TO THE FIELD

Bidding our farewells, we dispersed across the dominion. Those of us with private vehicles were given a few days to travel to our destination. Wide-eyed and intimidated, the four of us who had been assigned to Alberta postings arrived in Edmonton from Depot and were sequestered in barracks at K Division Headquarters. Our quarters there were similar to those we had just vacated, and our movements were carefully monitored through curfews and room inspections. We wondered if we would forever have to endure the harshly disciplined way of life we had suffered through during training.

After a few weeks of escorting prisoners, serving summonses and conducting minor investigations on behalf of outlying detachments, we were paraded in red serge before Assistant Commissioner Lloyd Bingham. An impressive man with blazing blue eyes, he conveyed to us the constant requirement for professionalism and devotion to duty. With the sting of Depot still in our beleaguered psyches, the commanding officer's message rang out as a stark prediction of our continuing monk-like existence.

I had just become part of a rigidly structured organization. The commissioner is the supreme head of the RCMP; a commanding officer, usually an assistant commissioner, is the chief executive of each province; and an officer commanding, a superintendent or inspector, is the head of what was referred to as a subdivision. Each province was divided into several geographical subdivisions, to which a number of detachments would report. Senior and junior non-commissioned officers (NCOs) were our direct and secondary supervisors. Even with the rigid cavalry-style structure, detachment commanders were given considerable autonomy with respect to day-to-day operations. They were subject to the regular scrutiny of section NCO staff sergeants, who roamed their subdivisions and reported to the officer commanding.

After a few weeks in Edmonton, I was posted to a town I'll call Willmore, where I would be the sole unmarried member of a seven-man detachment. I was excited and delighted when I learned that the town was nestled in the foothills of the Rocky Mountains. It had the reputation of being a busy detachment, a good place for a fledgling policeman to learn his law-enforcement craft. Packing my sparse belongings in my car, I headed west. The trip took about two hours, and my mind reeled with questions as I drove. Where would I live? Who would be my superior? Would I be accepted? I was attired in my best and only suit and tie, shoes shined and hair newly cut in the hope of making a good impression. As I neared the community, my stress intensified. Suddenly, it was in front of me—the red-brick building housing the detachment office and the quarters of the corporal in charge. I parked carefully in the parking lot and proceeded to the main entrance. The door was unlocked, and I entered. As I stood at the front counter, I could see a uniformed member sitting in what appeared to be the detachment commander's office. He did not acknowledge me. I cleared my throat to attract his attention. Glancing up, he seemed to comprehend my presence. Rising from the desk unsteadily, he promptly closed the office door. I was again alone in the detachment, standing at the counter for what seemed an eternity.

ACCELERATED PROMOTION

Corporal James Oliver Fripps was the senior single man living in barracks at Division Headquarters in Edmonton in the early '60s. For several years, he had assumed the weighty responsibility of organizing the annual regimental dinner. Jim had a penchant for living like a country squire, even though cloistered in barracks. His barrack room was opulent, like something one would find in a posh hotel. If you knew where to look, there was even a stocked bar. Being invited into Jim's quarters as a junior man meant you had arrived. Jim was highly respected for his intellect and renowned for his crackling wit.

On this particular occasion, he had done another exceptional job of setting up the regimental dinner and ensuring it went smoothly. Assistant Commissioner G.B. McLelland, the commanding officer, invoked the custom of his officers serving the meal to the men, which they did with aplomb.

During the debriefing of the event, the CO complimented Corporal Fripps on the splendid manner in which he had choreographed the evening. He went on to say he hoped that the corporal would be on hand for organizing the dinner the following year. Jim, with the usual twinkle in his eye, glanced at the CO and replied, "If it's all the same to you, Sir, next year, I would just as soon be a waiter!"

Finally, a police car drove into the parking lot, and a member emerged. He apologized and introduced himself as Bill McCoy, the senior constable. He seemed embarrassed, but showed me to my quarters, helped me with my luggage and took me for lunch. I enquired about the other member I had seen back at the office, but McCoy gave me no explanation.

As I settled into my work at the detachment and got to know the other members, I learned that the NCO I had initially encountered was an alcoholic who had been under the weather on the day of my arrival, at 10:00 a.m. Rather than confront me, he had shut the door to his office and made a phone call, presumably to McCoy. This NCO would have quite an impact on my early days at the detachment. Several nights after my arrival, I made my first liquor seizure, of which

I was justly proud. It was quite late when Constable McCoy and I returned to the office, and I was instructed to lock my seized exhibit in the NCO's office pending our return the following morning. Arriving early the next day to deal with my seized liquor, I discovered that two bottles of beer were missing from the carton. It appeared the alcoholic NCO had liberated a portion of my exhibits. As was the case in the good old days, this behaviour was overlooked. Constable McCoy told me to ignore the incident and replenished the open carton with the purchase of two identical bottles.

As my career unfolded I learned that many NCOs of this era suffered from alcoholism. While this was a common affliction among middle managers in many professions at the time, much of the excessive drinking within the RCMP was due to stress caused by inadequate personnel and long hours. There was a stark contrast between the discipline and compliance with the rules espoused in the training division and reinforced by management and the realities of detachment policing. Much of the blurring of lines between on- and off-duty behaviour was attributable to the lack of shift work at smaller outposts. Members were expected to be available to attend to any kind of emergency and were never truly off duty. Accordingly, we all tended to take advantage of spare moments when the phone didn't demand our attention. The unwritten philosophy was "work hard but play hard." Three hundred–hour work months were the rule rather than the exception, and this grinding workload encouraged some rule bending when it came to socializing on the job. It was not uncommon for on-duty members to drop in on a party if there were no demands for their services. In spite of this informality, calls were rarely missed and work assignments always completed. The countless examples of good and ethical police work far outnumbered the rare examples of neglect.

Thankfully, the imbibing NCO I had initially encountered was only there in the detachment commander's absence. When he returned, I learned I would serve under Corporal John Russell, a competent professional.

MOIETY

Back in the Jurassic era, circa 1960, serving members of the RCMP received a bonus each year, usually around Christmas. Affectionately referred to as a "moiety cheque," it usually amounted to $25 to $35 and was drained off what was then known as the Benefit Trust Fund. It seems like a pittance now, but it was a rather princely sum then, often used to bolster the supply of Christmas cheer in RCMP residences across the land.

I had just arrived in Willmore, fresh out of training. Six of the members there were well established and married. Then there was me, recipient of wisdom and knowledge from these half-dozen personal heroes on a daily basis. I was taking every precaution to avoid obvious mistakes and not make a nuisance of myself, and striving to establish my credibility with my co-workers.

It was early December, and on top of my $250 monthly pay cheque, the corporal conferred upon me my very first moiety cheque. In addition to this good news, I learned that there was to be a detachment Christmas dinner at one of the members' homes. Everyone was expected to attend. I arrived at the dinner party dressed to the nines. Everyone was gathered in the living room idly chatting.

Anxious to become involved, I made eye contact with one of the members and enquired in a rather loud voice what he planned to do with his moiety cheque. There was an instant, dead, cold silence. One of the wives asked, "Moiety cheque? What on earth is that?" Curiously, none of the wives, some of whom had been married to the members for years, had any knowledge of the moiety cheque.

The evening dragged on. Most left early. My brief career lay in tatters. I received the silent treatment for days and washed police cars for weeks. People sentenced to the gulag had better lives. Just when I had given up all hope and was contemplating applying to join foreign armies, my transgression was forgiven. Then there were weeks of fending off snide comments from members as my fame spread throughout the subdivision and further. It was a hard lesson learned. Never before had I inserted my foot so far in my mouth than on that lonely Christmas evening many years ago.

Formalized field training for recruits had not yet been introduced, so their indoctrination was left to the discretion of the detachment commander. Corporal Russell struck a perfect balance between providing necessary supervision and giving me sufficient latitude to develop independently. Additionally, I was fortunate to work with six seasoned veterans as I began to accumulate the skills, knowledge and wiles I would need in my law-enforcement career.

THE COMMUNITY OF Willmore was located squarely in the oil patch, with up to 20 oil rigs operating in the district at any one time. Each rig was a small industrial enclave headed up by a foreman, known as a tool push, and three drillers, each with a contingent of roughnecks working round-the-clock shifts. Approximately 24 people lived in bunk-houses at the isolated rig, which also had a mess hall doling out gourmet meals. Many of the rigs were classified as "tight holes," which meant security was strict and access to the site closely controlled. Rival drilling companies hired spies called scouts, who were paid large sums of money to infiltrate the rig site and gather information. Scouts would scale trees and view the premises with binoculars in an attempt to count the lengths of drill pipe, which would indicate how far down the rig was drilling. Scouts plied off-duty riggers with drinks and even cash to garner information. Occasionally, security staff would detect these spies and pursue them on Ski-Doos and four by fours in wild chases that sometimes ended with apprehension and assaults. It was an extremely dangerous lifestyle, filled with hard physical work and adventure.

Off-duty rig crews frequented bars and restaurants in town, leaving huge amounts of money and havoc in their wake. Any disturbances they caused invariably came to the attention of the RCMP, generating hours of work. The oil companies considered good relations with local police to be paramount, so their cooperation was a valuable tool. If off-duty employees created problems for the police, a well-placed word with the tool push would send the worker packing. Drill crews were aware of this and avoided confrontations with police during their sometimes raucous off-duty activities. Unexecuted warrants for transient rig employees were received from all parts of Canada, so regular patrols were made to the rigs to ensure fugitives were not part of the workforce. RCMP members were always welcomed on the rig site and often treated to a much-appreciated meal while conducting these patrols.

A major provincial highway crossed the town and detachment area, bringing many transients into Willmore. Constable Kenneth Giblin, one of the members of the highway patrol, possessed an uncanny ability to detect crime and criminals. As a result, he was often at the centre of potentially dangerous incidents. Highway patrol members routinely work alone and often find themselves far from backup. Most of them are acutely aware of the risks and use care and discretion when they find themselves in vulnerable positions. Giblin was fearless under any circumstances and seemed to have an invisible shield of protection. This was evident one night when he stopped two men driving down the highway. They looked nervous, so Giblin examined the car more thoroughly. Under the driver's seat, he discovered a sawed-off, double-barrelled shotgun, with two rounds in the firing chambers. Giblin arrested both men for possession of an illegal firearm. They each received sentences of six months in prison. Unhappy with the penalty, they appealed their sentence, at which time the appeal court doubled their incarceration to one year.

A short time later, we received a bulletin describing two American men sought for a recent murder. The armed fugitives were considered two of the most dangerous individuals at large in the northern USA and could be heading our way. Constable Giblin spotted a vehicle with American licence plates travelling through the area. After pulling the vehicle over and seeing two male occupants, he sensed danger and drew his revolver when he approached. Giblin saw drug paraphernalia inside the car, so with his gun still drawn, he handcuffed one man to the steering wheel. During the process, the other man tried to jump the constable. He was soundly smacked by the barrel of an RCMP .38 Special revolver and then handcuffed. Giblin then turned to the other culprit, who viciously kicked him. The constable released his assailant from the steering wheel, and the man was suddenly confronted by what he later referred to as a maniac in a Stetson hat. His only recollection was being knocked senseless and waking up in handcuffs. The pair was transported to the detachment, where a more thorough search uncovered an arsenal of illegal weapons in the vehicle. The fugitives were returned to the US and stood trial for three counts of murder. Giblin's bravery proved that the spirit of resoluteness and confidence displayed during the early years of the Force still lived on.

I had only been in the field for a few months when I was dispatched to my first sudden death. It was the dead of winter when a call was received from a concerned citizen who had not seen his neighbour for some time. The missing person was a solitary trapper who lived in an isolated cabin some miles from the nearest habitation. The temperature hovered around −30°F when I headed out to investigate. I approached the cabin at dusk and found a set of tracks leading off into the bush. Following the trail, I found the missing man lying dead beside a small lake. The circumstances were not suspicious, and the victim appeared to have died of natural causes while inspecting his trap line. I returned to the police car to contact the detachment via police radio. The corporal explained that the coroner had been informed but would not attend since the death seemed routine and the weather was frigid. An ambulance had been dispatched, and I was instructed to bring the body to an accessible location. The light was fading, casting a rather ominous and spooky aura over the scene. Hastily returning to the cabin, I located a toboggan and returned to the body, which was frozen solid, arms and legs akimbo, making it very difficult to move. I manoeuvred the body onto a toboggan and headed off to where I would meet the ambulance. The corpse caught on trees and slid off in the snow, and I was beginning to hear strange noises as darkness settled in. Visions of wolves competing for my charge danced in my brain. Finally, after wrestling the body through a half-mile of bush, I spotted the ambulance with the very welcome presence of the driver. Together we loaded the body in the ambulance and returned to town.

As is common in most small communities, the ambulance driver was both a close associate of the local detachment and a good friend. Our man, Tony Olio, not only drove the ambulance, but also ran the community funeral home. Wearing both these hats, Olio's path frequently intersected with that of detachment members. He was from a nearby coal-mining community and apparently had a reputation as a moonshiner. We were convinced that Olio had left his distilling career far behind him; however, we were to learn from RCMP Federal Enforcement investigators that he was under surveillance for being up to his old tricks. They had received intelligence that he was transporting his illicit spirits into the city in his hearse. On one of Olio's trips, the RCMP's Preventive Service Section, aka the liquor squad, intercepted him. They examined his hearse and found a large amount of home brew. A further search of Olio's residence revealed a commercial still. Our compatriot was arrested and charged with bootlegging. Shortly thereafter he appeared in local court to plead guilty and was levied a large cash fine. To his credit, he held no grudges. In fact, the following Sunday, Tony invited the entire detachment to his home for breakfast. Tony apologized for the error of his ways and hoped that it would not affect our professional and social relationship. The corporal deemed that he had paid his debt to society, and since we needed an undertaker and an ambulance driver, we continued on as if nothing had occurred. We were all slightly more vigilant, however, when it came to Tony's activities.

Garfield was our neighbouring detachment to the west, and it was staffed by two members. Corporal Roydon Porter was the detachment commander and a member of a distinguished RCMP family, almost Kennedyesque in the tragedies that had befallen it. The patriarch of the clan had been one of the Force's longest-serving commissioners. He was the son of a former assistant commissioner, whose lineage was directly connected to American president Zachary Taylor. The commissioner had sired three sons; one died in combat during the Second World War and a second was killed in a motor vehicle accident while serving with the RCMP. Roydon, the youngest and only surviving son, had also joined the Force. He made no secret of his distinguished background, but in spite of it his garrulous personality made him a favourite among his peers. His second man, Jack Fargey, was a senior constable awaiting his own promotion. The area they were responsible for was primarily wilderness, and Garfield was a generally placid mill community, which meant that these two experienced members only needed to deal with minor incidents. During the World Series, we expected them to appear at our detachment to watch the games on television, bringing with them a case of beer and a huge jar of peanuts.

A later encounter with a section NCO further elevated Corporal Porter's standing in the eyes of his co-workers. The role of a section NCO was to serve as the right-hand man of the officer commanding. Section NCOs were assigned a number of detachments to inspect regularly to ensure general policy compliance. Staff Sergeant "Snapper" John Nance, our section NCO, was married to the Force, lock, stock and barrel, and expected everyone else to be equally dedicated. An officious man, much impressed by his own importance, he expected complete subservience from his minions. Time meant nothing to him; it was not unusual for his detachment visits to begin in the evening, when he would demand that the detachment commander forgo his dinner to be on hand for his inspection of the premises.

One evening, he arrived on the doorstep of Corporal Porter, who was just closing up shop for the day. Staff Sergeant Nance informed Corporal Porter that he would be commencing his review of the detachment. The corporal looked at his watch and explained he was done for the day and would return to the office at eight o'clock the following morning.

BLUEBERRIES

While I was stationed at Willmore during the early '60s, the detachment consisted of seven members, four on district duties and three on traffic, with each unit supervised by a corporal. Corporal John Russell, in charge of the district, was the detachment commander, while Corporal Tetzloff supervised the traffic unit. There was a good rapport and healthy competition between the two units.

On long weekends, the detachment policy for major highways was one of "saturation." All units were directed onto the highway for as many hours as humanly possible—and longer. The objective was to reduce the carnage due to increased holiday traffic. One warm Victoria Day long weekend, all members and vehicles were on duty and patrolling the highway. As it happened, the two corporals had decided to team up to supervise. RCMP policy in that era demanded acute attention to uniform dress code, and these astute leaders had identified the proper wearing of kit as a priority. The uniform of the day was boots and breeches, brown tunics and Stetsons. The unwieldy Stetson had to be worn at all times when outside the cruiser.

As the corporals roamed their domain, they spotted Constable Rob Drucker out of his car making a vehicle check. Drucker was a folksy farm boy originally from the Ottawa Valley, who often had difficulty adhering to uniform regulations. It was obvious that he was hatless while making this vehicle check. The detachment commander decided to make an example of Drucker and waited until he had finished checking the vehicle.

The two NCOs pulled in behind the errant constable. Corporal Russell got out of his car and walked smartly over to Drucker and had a brief conversation, which ended rather abruptly. The corporal returned to his vehicle. Corporal Tetzloff, very interested in Drucker's reaction to the upbraid, queried the senior corporal, who looked dejected. "I demanded to know why he didn't have his Stetson on! He told me that it was not possible." "Why?" the corporal asked. "Because it's full of blueberries!" was his answer. It was completely logical to Drucker—and shows why supervisors sometimes pray for divine intervention.

He then promptly shut the door in Staff Sergeant Nance's face. Infuriated, Nance immediately phoned Superintendent Little, the officer commanding, disturbing him after hours. Nance explained how Corporal Porter had dismissed him at the doorstep and requested authority to proceed with disciplinary action. The officer commanding was very aware of Corporal Porter's dizzying connections within the high echelons of the Force. He astounded Nance by telling him to ignore the rebuff and start his inspection in the morning. This single brave action brought fame and glory to Corporal Porter from his detachment commander peers. It broke the reign of terror exercised by Staff Sergeant Nance and changed the oppressive working conditions that he had imposed throughout the subdivision.

During my first summer at Willmore, I was taken back to my youth when the exhibition came to town. Many of us have fond childhood memories of the excitement and magic of these travelling exhibitions. The presence of the big top in Yorkton always attracted hordes of people and required extra policing duties. I remember the midway manager's visits to my father's office. I had no idea why, but he always left gifts for the police and their families. The gifts took the form of free-ride tickets for the kids and certain "favours" for the adults. Amazingly, years later at my first posting, the same midway manager came to our town. I no longer cared for ride tickets, but I now learned that he had bottles of Crown Royal rye for each member of the detachment. It was unlikely that such luxuries would be bought on a policeman's salary, so we were delighted with the gifts. Looking back on it now, I am astounded that we were so naïve. There was only one reason for the generosity: our detachment was supposed to look the other way, particularly with respect to the girly shows and the games of chance on the midway. Several years later this same midway conglomerate was charged with offences surrounding inducements and even bribery of officials. During the enquiry into the company, their books were opened for scrutiny. There in black and white was a precise account of every free ride ticket and bottle of whisky given to each policeman, including my father and me and hundreds of other seemingly innocent officials. Although the gifts were minor, it made me realize how easily one can be compromised.

Two of the quickest ways of incurring instant discipline and, most likely, dismissal, was the loss of a prisoner and the mishandling of exhibits, specifically liquor exhibits. With money being so tight, it was forever tempting to direct the odd case of beer or unopened bottle of liquor to the back room rather than down the drain. In spite of the consequences if caught, some members gambled with fate by enjoying the fruits of their labour. It was not uncommon for careers to be ruined and bright futures dimmed through the discovery of a bottle of beer that did not get properly destroyed. Liquor exhibits had to be carefully inventoried and held pending the appeal period. When the time for disposal arrived, the local magistrate had to observe the destruction, signing a form testifying to this. The occasional magistrate viewed the relegation of sealed exhibits down the drain as draconian. In these cases the form would be signed with the justice conveniently absent during the destruction, or possibly even on hand to assist in the consumption. It was a classic example of the old adage "Don't get caught!" The improper handling of liquor exhibits persisted for years. It was typical of the era and no doubt tied to poor pay and long working hours. Exhibits are handled much more professionally in today's Force.

While there were no RCMP regulations forbidding members from socializing at local watering holes, detachment commanders would often discourage or forbid this activity in their local standing orders, which outlined expectations. But even when we were allowed to do so, entering bars and taverns while off duty was seldom a relaxing experience. Embittered clients and unsatisfied complainants tended to corner us, even if we were just trying to have a quiet beer. Members had to be constantly on their guard, and it was generally more trouble than it was worth. As a result, when we wanted to let off a little steam, we gathered at the local Legion or at private homes.

George and Edna Siebel owned a small mixed farm a short distance northeast of Willmore. They had become friends of several members, and it was not unusual for three or four of us to assemble there, accompanied by wives and girlfriends. The Siebels were wonderful hosts and their home was an oasis from the hectic pace of law enforcement. Anything that took place at the Siebels remained there. Edna always provided a delicious country meal, which was appreciated perhaps more by the only unmarried member. We all came to cherish this serene retreat, and our debt to the Siebels for their hospitality could never be properly repaid. We had a similar haunt at the Gordon and June Mitchell ranch just southwest of town, while Al and Manda Worthing, right in Willmore, also adopted the detachment and treated us like visiting royalty. It was as though these fine people had been preordained to provide a safe haven for all of us. In some cases they became proxy parents for homesick RCMP members and even provided marriage counselling when needed.

I found it eerie that these very welcome and necessary sanctuaries existed in every rural community in which I was stationed, and what is more, the personalities and settings were all very similar. As personnel changed at a detachment, incoming members gravitated to the same locations; however, it was not unusual for new members to discover other hospitable residents who offered similar places of refuge from public scrutiny. All of these kind and supportive citizens should have received recognition for the care and nurture they extended to the Mounted Police. Seldom were they publicly honoured; it seemed enough for them to enjoy our company and sometimes hilarious antics. Bulls got ridden, songs got sung and people got horse-troughed. Much *spiritus fermenti* was consumed and never a word uttered to the always curious public.

IN MANY COMMUNITIES across the country, local town and city councils have opted to have their own police force. At the same time, many of these communities contain an RCMP detachment. RCMP members police the outlying areas under the provincial contract agreement. They also have jurisdiction in the town, but defer to the local municipal police. In countless cases the local chief of police will call the RCMP in to assist when a serious crime occurs. Historically, RCMP members would be assigned these tasks with no worry or concern about who was going to pay for their hours. There existed a mutual understanding that RCMP members would assist whenever requested. This came to a grinding halt when the Force implemented overtime payment.

A five-man municipal force policed the town of Willmore. These officers received little formalized training, donning their blue uniforms and learning while they earned. They depended heavily upon RCMP assistance, particularly in the event of a serious crime. There was a healthy spirit of cooperation between Chief John MacDonald and Corporal Russell and none of the professional jealousy that permeated many RCMP–municipal police relationships. The chief was very aware of the advantage of having extra bodies at the local detachment, especially when transient oil-rig crews from outlying areas, flush with money, would come to town to drink at the two local hotels. Occasionally their antics would explode into melees in the downtown area, and the RCMP would be summoned to augment the town police. Much later in my service I would learn that this level of cooperation between forces was not always present.

One notorious individual in the district occasionally caught the attention of the police community. He was an interdicted person, banned by provincial statute from consuming or possessing liquor. I recall clearly his daunting physical size; his driver's licence described him as six foot six inches tall and 312 pounds. Occasionally, "Tiny" would ignore his interdicted status and consume large amounts of booze. One sunny summer's day he did just that and entered a local hotel's beverage room with his Metis common-law wife. Before the bartenders could alert the police, someone hollered, "Squaw man!" and all hell broke loose. The town police were called and, realizing who was involved, asked for RCMP assistance. When the Mounties arrived, the hotel looked as though a cyclone had hit it. Windows were broken, chairs lay out on the main street and injured bodies were strewn on the ground, while the assailant was still holed up inside the bar. Slim Gordon of the town police sidled up next to the giant and coaxed him out onto the street. Gordon, a tall, rangy cowboy, ordered Tiny into a police car, but Tiny declined. Slim took a little hop and placed his target in a headlock. The titan simply swung his arm and slammed Gordon against the car, where he crumpled to the ground with several broken ribs. Rob Drucker, one of the RCMP members, had a measure of rapport with Tiny from past encounters and spoke to him calmly. After some persuasion, Tiny meekly followed Drucker into the police cruiser. This incident exemplifies why the town police relied upon the RCMP and is just one of countless times I experienced when respect for the RCMP uniform helped to settle a dispute peacefully.

As the sole single man at the detachment, I lodged in the barracks for $15 a month. However, the privilege came with some disadvantages. Once in a while I was asked to babysit the detachment commander's children. I was compensated for this service with occasional and much-appreciated home-cooked meals. The other disadvantage was having to answer the phone after hours. For a while after my arrival at the detachment, another member would accompany me to after-hours calls, but as I became more experienced, I responded to calls alone, much to the relief of my married co-workers.

Once I received a 3:00 a.m. phone call from the town police. An intoxicated man was in custody at their office, but refused to go into the cells without a fight. I dressed in uniform and headed over to the town office. When the recalcitrant arrestee observed an RCMP member enter the office, he immediately entered the cells on his own. In his drunken logic, he explained that he would comply for a Mountie, but not for any blankety-blank town cop.

THE CRIMINAL CODE includes many obscure provisions. Among its many sections and paragraphs is a portion forbidding bestiality. It is a criminal offence for a Canadian to have sexual relations with an animal. Bill McCoy seemed to have a vested interest in this part of the statute, as though he was assuming personal responsibility to protect all animals from human amorous intent. As it happened, the remote far north of our detachment area could have been used for the setting of the movie *Deliverance*, and a few local residents wouldn't have been out of place in that bizarre film. Among them was a bachelor sheep rancher. Constable McCoy had received intelligence that the man was having relations with his woolly ewes, a blatant contravention of the Criminal Code. Bill was determined to catch the culprit *in flagrante delicto*, so when we had reason to be in the area, it was always on his mind.

One day Constable McCoy told me to be ready to depart for the area before day-break the following morning, as we were going to place the good shepherd under surveillance. I was not overly enthusiastic about getting up early to travel to this out-of-the-way location, but as the subordinate I was ready the following morning to accompany my partner. When we arrived, we abandoned the police car and thrashed our way through heavy underbrush to arrive at the scene of a possible crime. As we lay on the wet ground awaiting developments, I queried Constable McCoy as to who our target might be corrupting if in fact he had a sheep for a girlfriend. Bill looked at me askance, remarking that I was one sick puppy. After several hours of patient observation, we abandoned surveillance and went on to grander pursuits. We were never able to catch the shepherd in the act. He and his sheep continued to lead an uninterrupted and perhaps blissful life.

I was soon to learn of a much more troubling case of man's capacity for depravity in a small community in the eastern portion of our detachment area. A distraught woman in her 30s arrived at the detachment wishing to speak with a member. She told Constable McCoy that she had been sexually abused by her father when she was a preteen. A lengthy and sensitive investigation ensued, revealing that not one, but four daughters from this family had been sexual abuse victims. There were three sets of two sisters who were close in age, each pair about five years apart. The eldest sister had just learned the youngest girls were about to be victimized and approached the detachment in the hope that police intervention would prevent further offences. I was horrified as I followed the senior constable through the complex steps of the investigation. When all the data had been assembled, the father was confronted with the evidence. Amazingly, he admitted to victimizing four of his daughters and confirmed his intent to assault the remaining two. He justified his crime by stating that a father needed to properly introduce his daughters to the physical act of sex. Equally shocking was the fact that his wife had full knowledge of what was going on and supported her husband in his twisted premise of sex education. The father was arrested and charged with multiple counts of incest. Much to the disappointment of his daughters and the investigators, the court sentenced him to only four years' imprisonment. To those of us who were directly involved in bringing this heinous offence before the court, this sentence made it appear as though society regarded the crimes as almost acceptable.

My initial three-year stint on detachment duty was perhaps the best grounding that any young man could have asked for during that era. The variety of police work I experienced was nothing short of astounding, and I had the best of coaching from all six senior members. Percy Keyes, the magistrate, was a former member of the RCMP who did not suffer fools gladly. If I erred presenting my evidence in court, he would openly express his dissatisfaction. Calling me into his office at the conclusion of court, Magistrate Keyes would debrief me, explaining where I had gone astray and how I could improve my performance.

The area policed by the detachment consisted of large ranches, marginal backwoods settlements, oil fields, vast foothills, parkland, a Metis colony and abandoned coal-mine communities. Each of these presented their own law-enforcement challenges, ranging from minor thefts and break-ins to murder. Life's ironies often became evident in the course of law enforcement. Ed Zerba was an oilfield worker whose marriage had failed due to his transient lifestyle. Zerba frequently became delinquent in his support payments, which resulted in his ex-wife laying charges against him. On two occasions Zerba was arrested in BC and held, awaiting the arrival of a police escort. Both times, I was detailed to bring him back. The escort involved long periods of return travel, both by road and air, which gave me the opportunity to get to know Ed and precipitated a kind of offbeat friendship and rapport between us. Ed was an infamous oilfield derrick driller and a roustabout. He had a reputation as a fighter and was physically intimidating, which earned him the respect of his peers.

Several months after the delinquent husband had been released after his court appearance, a call came into the detachment at 3:00 a.m. from the concerned parents of three girls who had been seen partying with a number of roughnecks from local rigs. The party was taking place at a remote location outside of town and the underage girls were apparently being fed liquor. The senior constable and I patrolled to the area where we discovered a large bonfire, several men and the wayward girls. We approached the group with the intention of seizing the liquor and arresting the men for contributing to juvenile delinquency. Four of the men challenged us, and we realized, short of drawing our weapons, that we were in danger of losing control of the situation. Suddenly, Ed Zerba, my former prisoner and travelling partner, appeared out of the darkness. He stood next to us, informing the culprits they would have to deal with him also. Intimidated, the men backed down, allowing us to carry on with our seizures and arrests. Had it not been for Ed, we could have been seriously injured. Some time later, just before I was transferred, I happened to be in one of the local hotel beverage rooms. I spotted Ed sitting at an adjacent table and sent a round over to him. He joined me, wishing me luck at my new posting and remarked that he had always been treated fairly and with respect by the detachment.

Members of the Mounted Police were frequently expected to work alone, often in situations that should have called for additional personnel. Single-man detachments frequently depended on local citizenry as backup. One evening, long after midnight, I responded to a call from a lonely hamlet located on a secondary road deep in the wilderness. It was a dusty, 40-mile trip. After resolving a family dispute in the community, I wended my lonely way back to town. Encountering a car parked on the road, I stopped to conduct a check. Inside were four young men, well known to the detachment for creating disturbances. As I stood next to the driver, I could smell alcohol in the vehicle. I opened the rear door and spied an open case of beer. As I reached in to seize it, one of the occupants stepped on my hand. The four jumped out of the car, swearing and cursing, and I suddenly found myself in a dangerous and vulnerable position. Interestingly, the option of drawing my weapon did not occur to me, even though I was running through options for self-preservation. The four men had surrounded me and I was expecting the worst when another car drove up. The driver was Peter Pambrun, the older brother of one of the offenders and a frequent client of the RCMP. Peter stood in front of me and faced my challengers. When his brother challenged him, he delivered a strong right cross to the chin, knocking his sibling off his feet. The other three immediately backed away. Peter told them that it did not appear to be a fair fight. He said that he had always been treated right by the Mounted Police and would not stand by and let one member be outnumbered. I seized the liquor, charged all four with its illegal possession and carried on. Word of Pambrun's assistance was relayed to the corporal, who in turn thanked my saviour.

EARLY IN MY service, I was involved in an incident that starkly illustrated the importance of following the lofty phrase in our oath of office: "Without Fear, Favour, or Affection." In the wilderness south of Willmore, Oscar Swedberg had founded a prosperous logging operation. He employed a large number of men and ran his company like the Ponderosa Ranch on the television show *Bonanza*. Many seasonal employees and their families lived in company cabins on the property. Oscar was a benevolent employer and ensured his hands received ample benefits and pay, but he was fervently anti-union and fought efforts on the part of outside labour unions to organize his workers. Oscar strongly supported law and order and cooperated with the detachment whenever required. Our personnel would frequently enjoy meals in the camp mess hall when on patrol in the area.

In 1964 there was considerable labour union activity in the forest industry in northern Alberta. Two representatives from a large labour union visited the logging operation. We began to receive complaints about the men verbally and physically harassing workers in attempts to unionize them. One complaint indicated the two strong-arms had entered one of the cabins and assaulted an occupant. Constable McCoy and I were dispatched to intercept the aggressive pair. We encountered them on the logging company's property, informed them they were trespassing and confronted them about the assault. Their response was anything but neighbourly; they called us a couple of hick queen's cowboys and told us to get lost and leave them to their union business. I opened the passenger door, pulled the occupant out, threw him to the ground and arrested him for assault and trespassing. During the heat of battle I may have uttered a derogatory comment. The driver came peacefully, and we escorted them to the detachment where they were released on bail.

I soon learned how quickly brown stuff flows downhill. Apparently our confrontation had been reported to national union headquarters. In turn, a complaint was registered in Ottawa with the commissioner, alleging the union reps had been called "Goddamn Commies." The complaint flowed from the commissioner to the commanding officer to the officer commanding the subdivision. Our section NCO, Staff Sergeant Nance, was dispatched immediately to our detachment to investigate and obtain statements. When he heard Nance was on his way, Corporal Russell counselled me, noting that members would never call anyone a communist. Realizing I may have done exactly that, I was somewhat confused by my corporal's direction. He reiterated, "You did not make that statement!" I concluded that he must know more than I did. When Nance arrived, I obeyed the corporal and denied any knowledge of such a statement. The staff sergeant accepted my denial with some suspicion and departed. The matter was not pursued, but after the fact, Corporal Russell and I had a lengthy discussion about the hazards of emotional outbursts when making arrests.

The topography for hundreds of miles south of Willmore is mountain wilderness, with fast-running creeks flowing down steep ridges into secluded, heavily wooded valleys. Even if one follows the game trails that criss-cross the terrain, walking in this vast area can be very challenging. Early in the 20th century, several coal-mining communities flourished in the area. When the mines were exhausted, people relocated, abandoning these towns. Several of them became true ghost towns, inhabited only by a few ancient, rugged individuals who refused to leave. In the '30s, the settlements were in their heyday, complete with lively social activity. During one rowdy Saturday evening dance in one of these communities, a disagreement broke out between two men over a woman. One of the men broke into a house and fired a handgun several times, seriously wounding three people. The culprit ran off into the wilderness. Police were called and a search conducted. They knew the identity of the gunman but couldn't locate him. Although he was a local resident, he was never seen again. An investigation was pursued for several years, but the file remained open and inactive.

In 1962, while making his way through the rough terrain surrounding the old town, a hunter noticed what he thought was an unusual mushroom sitting at the base of a large Douglas fir. When he got closer and picked it up he realized it was a human skull. Holding the skull in front of him, he ran several hundred yards through the bush to his hunting partner. Totally out of breath and on the brink of collapse, he tried to explain what had happened. The hunter apparently had a heart condition, so his partner was more concerned with his friend's medical situation than the skull. They emerged from the bush and called the RCMP for assistance. Constable McCoy and I immediately patrolled to the scene. Once we had tended to the hunter, we retraced his steps to find the skull. Amazingly, he was able to take us directly to the site. The first thing that gave us some concern was the obvious bullet hole in the skull. When we examined the area around the fir tree, we found a watch, along with a .32 calibre automatic pistol. The scene was mapped and photographed, and the two items were sent to Identification section for further tests. The revolver was too badly corroded to retrieve any serial numbers, but the watch was traced to the same individual who had been suspected of shooting the three victims 30 years before. We surmised that he had run off into the woods, stopped at this location and committed suicide. I felt considerable satisfaction at successfully concluding a file that had remained open for three decades. It also revealed to me how long the Force persevered in cases of violence.

BEFORE EMERGENCY RESPONSE TEAMS ————————————

It was the very early spring of 1964. Andy, an elderly trapper who resided alone in a small cabin in the tiny settlement of Entrance, Alberta, had not been seen by his neighbours for some time. Andy's concerned landlord went to the cabin and knocked. The response was a shot through the door with what appeared to be a .22 calibre bullet. Hinton RCMP were called and responded immediately. They approached the cabin cautiously from the rear, stood to one side of the door, knocked and identified themselves. Another shot rang out, and a bullet came through the door. The RCMP made additional calls to the cabin's occupant, who responded by firing more shots. The two RCMP members retreated and considered their options.

The RCMP subdivision HQ was telephoned and informed of the incident. Reinforcements from Edson, a nearby detachment, were dispatched, along with Staff Sergeant Gordon Blye, the west section senior NCO. The personnel cordoned off the scene to ensure the neighbours' safety and waited for help to arrive. The two additional RCMP members and the senior staff sergeant arrived later in the day. Emergency response gear was not readily available, but Blye had acquired a US Army helmet and bulletproof vest. Several times, the occupant of the cabin was hailed and responded by firing his gun. During this exchange, the weapon being used suddenly escalated to a larger calibre rifle, which was much louder and did considerably more damage to the sides of the cabin. Obviously the situation had just become more dangerous.

Staff Sergeant Blye had also brought with him a tear-gas gun and projectiles. Tear gas was unfamiliar to the members involved and indeed rarely used by police personnel, particularly in rural settings. Since it was impossible to approach the cabin, HQ was contacted for authorization to use tear gas; however, this authorization was denied because of the age of the occupant and the danger of fire. Smoke could be seen rising from the chimney of the dwelling. The "task force" decided that if the smoke could be blocked off, the resident might be forced to exit. The small contingent of police officers crawled through the dense bush around the cabin to get closer to the building. A decision had been made to lift a pail with a long pole in an attempt to drop it over the chimney. As Staff Sergeant Blye was suitably attired in combat gear, he volunteered to block the smoke hole.

The RCMP members were dressed in heavy storm coats and wore their holstered sidearms underneath. They had removed their revolvers from their holsters and placed them in the large pockets of the storm coats for easier accessibility. As they took up a position close to the cabin, the staff sergeant was intent on setting up his attack on the chimney. One of the members approached the boss with a problem. As he was struggling through the bush, his revolver had slipped out of his pocket and became lost. Staff Sergeant Blye took a deep breath, rolled his eyes and instructed the member to retrace his steps in the hope of locating the missing gun.

Newly focused on the problem at hand, Blye slithered along on his belly to get as close to the chimney as possible. The rest of the contingent watched with bated breath as the staff sergeant was now completely out in the open and vulnerable to the firepower from the cabin. Slowly the pail on the end of the pole was inched toward its target. Just as it was about to be slipped down over the chimney, the pail dropped on the roof and bounced several times to the ground, making quite a racket. Almost simultaneously, a shot rang out from the cabin and a bullet roared through the cabin wall, splintering timber. Blye lay quietly flat on the ground. Much to the disbelief of his troops, he tried once again to place the pail over the chimney. This time he was successful. Andy, the elderly occupant, came to the door several times to "air out" the premises, but no amount of persuasion could entice him to exit the cabin.

Darkness was now approaching, and the incident was at a stalemate. The vehicles' headlights were used to light the scene throughout the night. A long, cold vigil in sub-zero temperatures greeted the five frustrated police officers as they guarded the scene. Finally, dawn arrived along with several media personnel from the nearest city, hot on the story of the "Mad Trapper" under siege in the wilds of Alberta. The RCMP members gathered around to determine their next step. Suddenly, the door to the cabin opened and out sauntered the elderly man, headed for the woodpile. Two RCMP officers sprinted toward him. When they confronted him, Andy looked up at the two exhausted policemen and stated, "Am I ever glad to see you guys, somebody has been prowling around my cabin trying to break in!" The policemen looked at each other in amazement.

Two rifles—a .22 calibre and a .300 Savage bolt action—were found inside the cabin, along with ample ammunition. Andy had been lying on his bed with the rifles, firing randomly at any noise he heard. He was declared mentally unfit and spent the rest of his days in a rest home. The daily city newspaper published a photo of the scene with Andy being taken into custody. Some days later, the detachments involved received memos of reprimand from subdivision HQ. Apparently the investigating officers appeared in the news photo without appropriate uniform headgear. No compliments were forthcoming for a job well done. And the lost revolver? It was found in the snow and safely returned to its rightful owner.

LAW ENFORCEMENT IN Canada has changed dramatically within a single generation. In 1962, the members of the police community of Willmore gathered one sunny July morning at a restaurant next to the bank on Main Street. Five policemen, including three RCMP members, fully dressed in the uniform of the day, but unarmed, sipped coffee and chatted in the vinyl booths that morning. The two municipal members present were also in uniform, also unarmed. Sidearms were rarely worn during the day, and none were evident. It did not occur to any of them that they would be quite helpless in the event of an armed robbery at the bank next door. If those same police officers were meeting in that same restaurant in 2013, all would be armed with nine millimetre automatic pistols and wearing bulletproof vests. Tasers and tear gas would be readily available on their utility belts, and they would carry personal hand-held police radios. Shotguns and rifles would be immediately accessible in their police cars.

The RCMP resisted tactical uniform changes for some years, but as the number of murdered policemen across Canada increased, so did the demands for more effective protection. There was a period of time during the transition when the RCMP actually forbade members from wearing bulletproof vests that they had purchased on their own. As early as 1975, I was part of a study group at headquarters in Ottawa examining the possibility of adopting an automatic pistol over the standard .38 Special revolver. The resistance to change at that point was insurmountable, as too many senior officers refused to permit the Force to "go the way of American law enforcement." It took many years for RCMP management to finally realize that the protection of members and a change to more effective armament was imperative.

CHAPTER 5

TEMPORARY POSTINGS, TEMPORARY TRAUMA

During my time at Willmore, I served temporarily at two adjacent detachments. Mountain View was located in one of Canada's national parks, and Mofort was a small rural community north of Willmore. Both were brief tours, but I learned a great deal. Sadly, I also worked under two more detachment commanders suffering from alcoholism.

I arrived in Mountain View during the summer of 1962, and my experience there can only be described as bittersweet. Since the detachment was located in a national park, members were required to wear red serge while on duty. The detachment commander was Corporal Wallace Warren, a fearsome-looking man sporting a large handlebar mustache. A Second World War veteran, he proudly displayed two rows of campaign medals on his left breast. When I reported for duty, he projected a distinct aura of authority and even intimidation. As I stood at attention, he rattled off his expectations, informing me I was to appear before him after lunch in red serge.

After lunch, I presented myself as ordered. Inspecting me thoroughly, the corporal expressed his concern about sending me downtown in red serge. His worry was due to my height, and he told me to keep moving because the dogs might mistake me for a fire hydrant and piss on my shiny high brown boots. He then instructed me to remove my spurs and don a set of green coveralls. After complying, with some puzzlement, I was told that as junior man my first duty of the day was to go to the liquor store and purchase a case of beer, the coveralls being my disguise. That errand set the tone and routine for the rest of the summer. This paragon of authority turned out to be a paper tiger driven by a great thirst. Routinely, the day-shift members and the odd local civilian could be found ensconced in a barrack room drinking beer. I felt a sense of impending disaster permeating the work environment.

One afternoon, with the detachment entrance unlocked and no one tending the counter, the day-shift members gathered in a small room for a beer. There was a timid rap on the door leading to our retreat. Corporal Warren commanded, "Enter!" Standing at the opened door was Superintendent Little, the officer commanding the subdivision. While we all froze in terror, Little's response was apologetic. He explained he had driven out from the city for the day. An avid golfer, he requested the free RCMP golf passes issued to the detachment by a famed local golf resort. Corporal Warren, breathing a sigh of relief, immediately obliged him, and Superintendent Little departed without a word of concern. Had the superintendent exercised his responsibilities as a manager and taken us to task, perhaps what happened later could have been averted and Corporal Warren's career saved.

HARLEY HEAVEN

As I face my 70th year, the sting of embarrassment has faded to the extent that I can now share this incident. Part of the Mountain View detachment fleet was a Harley Davidson police motorcycle. Because there were no members authorized to operate the bike, it languished unused in the detachment garage. I had long been a closet motorcyclist and wished mightily that I might one day even command my own police bike.

One glorious summer afternoon, I noted that the downtown area seemed awash with attractive damsels, as was frequently the case. The detachment commander had left me to my own devices. It occurred to me that one quick patrol astride a police motorcycle in red serge would give me a high profile that might lead to an innocent dalliance. In addition, it would elevate the general traffic-enforcement identity of the detachment. As I entered the detachment garage, the splendour and majesty of the police motorcycle was undeniable. The key had been hanging very vulnerably in the corporal's office. I turned it in the ignition and the Harley thundered to life. I quickly shut it off, cowed somewhat by the power of the beast.

As I returned to the detachment with the key, the vision of myself upon the Harley returned. The dark side won, and I returned to the garage, climbed onto the cycle and turned the key. As it rumbled, I wrestled with the clutch and shift lever, feeling more comfortable all the time. Opening the garage doors, I slowly and carefully teetered out onto the street. As I approached 10 miles per hour, I gained more and more confidence. The bike seemed to stabilize as I approached 15 miles per hour.

As I neared my first intersection, I realized it was time to apply the brakes. Sadly, I had not been briefed as to the importance of removing spurs while on motorcycle patrol. Spurs are very useful to guide a horse; however, they tend to get caught on a motorcycle, which is precisely what occurred next. I tried to put my foot out to balance the bike as it came to a halt, but my spur had become entangled and refused to release my balancing foot. Suddenly I was lying on the road under 1,500 pounds of iron that was patiently thumping away at an idle.

I was very disappointed at the lack of assistance from the public. I lay on my side in my scarlet tunic under the ticking Harley, as passing motorists honked. It seemed to take an eternity to work my way loose from this iron beast, though it was probably just seconds. I managed to return the Harley to its upright position and pushed the motorcycle back to the detachment. Meanwhile, several young women drove by, waving and giggling. When I finally got the bike back into the garage, the corporal was there to greet me. Once again I found myself in fatigues, washing police cars and doing general chores around the detachment. It took some time to work myself back into uniform. When I did, the corporal thought it appropriate that I spend much of my shift on foot patrol, meeting the trains and greeting older ladies as they disembarked. A couple of them asked if there were any local RCMP members who were truly mounted. One of them seemed offended by my rather curt response.

One sunny summer day as the afternoon waned, the day shift migrated to Corporal Warren's quarters, situated behind the office. Two members were present along with the corporal, his wife and a local civilian. Corporal Warren was well into his cups and had donned a custom-made, western gun holster containing his .45 calibre revolver adorned with pearl handles. Without notice, Warren drew the revolver, spun the cylinder, snapped it back in place, and aimed the weapon at the civilian, pulling the trigger. One of the more quick-thinking members lunged, seized the gun and disappeared into the kitchen. While there, he checked the revolver, which contained a live round. It was only by sheer luck that a civilian wasn't murdered that day. The corporal had evidently got it in his mind that the guest had designs on his wife, and the horrifying incident may have been Warren's drunken way of warning the man off.

As was almost always the case, the incident was buried. Feeling jaded by the questionable manner in which this situation was handled, I returned to my home detachment in Willmore. Soon I learned that matters had gone from bad to worse in Mountain View. Corporal Warren's behaviour had deteriorated, causing one of the members to register a complaint. It was the beginning of the end for the detachment commander. He was relieved of his command and eventually retired, medals intact but reputation in tatters.

My second temporary posting was during the winter of 1963, when I worked at the Mofort detachment. There, I was saddened to witness the mistreatment of local First Nations people and how it was even sanctioned by statute. On occasion I observed Corporal Brothers, the Mofort detachment commander, travelling to a local Cree reserve and randomly pulling into a residence. He would enter the home, without a warrant and sometimes forcibly. If open liquor was found, it would be seized and the occupants charged and often arrested. The Indian Act, an antiquated federal statute, prohibited liquor in dwelling houses on a reserve.

As shocking as this scenario was, it happened routinely all over Canada on First Nations reserves until the discriminatory sections of the act were repealed in the 1970s. Frequently children witnessed their parents being arrested and taken away. Because the dependants could not be left alone, they too would be taken into custody by social agencies. Entire families were traumatized by something as innocuous as a six-pack of beer. Seeing the uniformed federal police force as the invaders of their homes, Native children grew up fearing and hating the RCMP. Witnessing this arbitrary and intolerant enforcement policy profoundly affected my ideas about First Nations policing.

In spite of his intolerance, oppressive tactics toward aboriginal people and bad temper, Corporal Brothers taught me a lot. He was well-versed in policy and ensured my investigations were thorough and concise. However, as was the case with many of my initial NCOs, I also learned much about how things ought not to be done.

One morning Corporal Brothers told me he was off to the city to visit some of his cronies. As he departed in one of the police vehicles, he said that if anyone asked where he was, I was to say he was off in the district on police business. He failed to return that day, and there was no sign of him the day after. On the third morning, I received a call from Staff Sergeant Sangster in RCMP headquarters in Edmonton. He wished to speak with the corporal, and when I stated that he was currently out of the office on police business he accused me of not knowing where my detachment commander was. Knowing Staff Sergeant Sangster did not suffer fools gladly, I was taken aback. He went on to explain, with little patience and a razor's edge in his voice, that one of our detachment vehicles was parked in the Division Headquarters lot with four inches of snow on it and had not been moved for two days. He suspected the corporal was somewhere other than "in the district conducting police work" and told me to find him forthwith and direct him to report back to Division Headquarters. With these instructions, he hung up the phone.

GUIDANCE ON ATTENDING SCENES OF CRIME

During my tenure at Mofort detachment I was nearing three years of service and had attained a certain comfort level in my law-enforcement career. It might even be fair to say some complacency had settled in, and perhaps this is the reason I ran afoul of my detachment commander. As a matter of routine in a small two-person operation, the office was closed on Saturday afternoons and Sundays. In my capacity as second man I was not free of all obligations and had to be available for calls, and I received a call at home late one Saturday afternoon.

Someone had broken into a farm residence some 20 miles from town. I asked the complainant a few cursory questions, assuring him we would be out to see him the following Monday. There must have been some guilt pangs, as I attended the office to type out a complaint describing the incident and left it on the corporal's desk.

On Sunday I received another call, this time from my corporal who had been in the office to read incoming complaints. He ordered me to report to the detachment forthwith. The tone of his voice told me something was amiss, so I hied over there. The corporal demanded to know why I had not attended the scene of the reported crime. Confronted with a thundering barrage of demeaning comments, I failed to cobble together any kind of a rebuttal. The corporal concluded by ordering me to return to my quarters, get into uniform and patrol to the farm immediately to commence an investigation. Routinely, when called out after hours, our uniform consisted of "straight blues," which were ordinary pants with a yellow stripe, uniform shirt and tunic. However, in this case, as part of the punishment, I was ordered to wear the uniform of the day, which included breeches and high brown boots. It's safe to say that I never again neglected to attend the scene of a break and enter.

Although an example of the kind of personalized service each and every complaint and citizen received, it exemplified how little regard managers paid to hours worked. In years to come, with the advent of overtime, detachment commanders were forced to make difficult decisions about reducing levels of service to the public. The changes had to have an impact on public cynicism regarding their police. As in so many other professions, the days of "house calls" were numbered.

Panic-stricken, I began phoning locations where I thought the boss might be lurking. As I searched, it occurred to me that anyone who would take a police car into the city, blatantly park it in plain sight and go on a bender was either blindly arrogant or patently stupid. Eventually I located the absentee corporal and explained his situation, leaving him to his own devices. He immediately contacted Staff Sergeant Sangster, assuring him he was returning to his post. I suspect the phone lines were smoking when the subdivision NCO was done with the corporal. He showed up at the detachment a couple of hours later looking somewhat worse for wear.

SHORTLY AFTER MY arrival in Mofort, the detachment commander departed on annual leave, placing Jim Foreman, the senior constable, in charge. He was a capable, well-respected individual with sufficient service and qualifications for promotion and appointment to his own command. Jim, along with his charming wife, Lil, and their two children, adopted me and insisted that I share in their activities. There was a small highway patrol adjacent to the detachment, but located in separate quarters. The detachment itself was a small structure within NCO quarters. Both highway patrol members were single, and the three of us boarded with another family in a large home.

One evening, I was invited to Jim Foreman's home for dinner. Everyone in the household was excited, as they had just ordered a brand new family car—a 1963 Chrysler Cordoba hardtop. Following a pleasant evening, I returned to my boarding house. At about two o'clock in the morning, I was awakened by my landlady explaining a call had just come in reporting a serious motor vehicle accident on the highway, a short distance from town. When I phoned Jim's residence to alert him, Lil told me he was currently out on a call. I was puzzled, as he had not contacted me to accompany him. Already dressed, I roused the highway patrol members, informing them I was on my way and would meet them at the scene. When I arrived there, I saw the usual chaos and debris of a highway accident. As I got out of my vehicle, I was shocked to see that a detachment patrol car was part of the accident scene. Then a witness approached me, saying that there was a body in the ditch near the vehicles. As I made my way down the ditch, to my horror, I saw the body was clad in an RCMP shirt. It was Jim Foreman. The highway patrol members arrived soon after. Equally shocked by my discovery, they took control of the scene and began the investigation.

As the story unfolded, we learned that Jim had received a call from a long-time informant offering some information of value, and they agreed to meet on the highway. Jim had parked his police car in front of the informant's vehicle. Both men were standing in front of the police car when a speeding vehicle on the same side of the highway came over the crest of the hill. It collided with the rear of the informant's vehicle, which struck the police car. Jim took the full brunt of the collision. He was thrown some 50 feet into the ditch and was killed instantly. The informant was injured, as was the driver of the colliding vehicle. The driver was found to be impaired at the time and was charged accordingly, but whatever penalty he paid could not restore Jim's life.

Within hours, there was a cadre of senior management, coroners and identification personnel at the scene. I was tasked with two stressful duties. First, I was to make an official identification of the body at the morgue. Second, in the absence of the detachment commander, it would be my responsibility to notify Lil. This was one of the most difficult experiences of my young life. Not being particularly religious, I had seldom put much stock in the utility of members of the cloth, but I quickly realized that in a situation like this, there is no more valuable asset. The local minister accompanied me to the Foremans' residence and virtually relieved me of my burden. I would be forever grateful to him for his expertise and compassion. The entire experience left me shaken and confused. The subsequent regimental police funeral in Edmonton was one of the largest ever conducted in the province, as members from all over Canada came to pay their respects.

After my tenure at Mofort ended, I returned to Willmore. The strong, upbeat atmosphere at my home detachment had also changed. Corporal Russell had been promoted and transferred and was replaced by a much less talented individual. And there was something else in the air—a pervasive uneasiness among the members. I learned that in my absence a married constable and his wife had fostered an errant 16-year-old girl in their home. Selected as community role models, they had been asked to act as mentors to her. While the girl was under his care, the constable had engaged in a sexual relationship with her, impregnating her while his own wife was giving birth in the hospital. The girl subsequently disclosed her condition to a local minister, who reported it to some local RCMP members. It appeared that no one at the detachment was going to take any action, even though a criminal offence had been committed if the allegations were substantiated. The atmosphere was oppressive; the more junior members felt the incident should not and probably could not be smothered. We believed the volatile situation had to be divulged to our superiors in subdivision headquarters. It plagued my conscience for several days until I made a decision. During a prisoner escort trip to Edmonton, I met with a senior officer. With great trepidation, I told him about the potentially explosive situation. He assured me the matter would be attended to and ordered me to return to the detachment.

The very next day, senior management arrived and conducted interviews that substantiated the allegations. Within days the offending member was transferred and his family relocated. Concerned about adverse publicity if this member were charged criminally, the Force offered him a choice of resigning or facing orderly room and criminal prosecution. The member promptly resigned, realizing he had been spared from disgrace and probably prison. Very soon after, all members of the detachment were assembled by the investigating inspector and given a stern lecture on loyalty to the Force. Management made it clear they were aware senior members had knowledge of the heinous transgression, yet failed to carry out their obligations to the Force and the public. With the Force still fearing the potential of scandal, the matter was concluded.

Sadly, this was another example of the double standard of that era. Integrity and principles were compromised to preserve the "good name" of the organization. Even today, there are still those within the RCMP who would do anything to cover up such misconduct, but there are many more members willing to speak up against it. With the advent of instant media attention and public expectation of professionalism from police forces, it is far less likely that such behaviour would be tolerated today.

Detachment morale never fully recovered from this catastrophe. The new corporal, who had not been involved, did little to improve matters. The incident remained under wraps, and because the community miraculously remained oblivious there was minimal backlash.

During my last year at Willmore, I met and married Lorraine. Many of us from this era were ill-equipped to make what was perhaps the most important decision of our young lives. Lorraine was trying to escape a dysfunctional home and a father who constantly struggled with alcoholism. I was responding to raging hormones and hoping to escape a cold existence in a single man's room in the back of the detachment. Marriages based on such shaky premises were not uncommon in the RCMP. These relationships could move in two directions: couples either grew together over time or grew apart. Sadly, our marriage would eventually disintegrate.

BEFORE THE 1970S, the RCMP was primarily a WASP organization, reflecting the power base of Canadian society. The words in our oath of office, "Without Fear, Favour or Affection," challenged members daily, and I strove to apply them. Yet, despite noble efforts by many to achieve this lofty goal, favouritism sometimes occurred. During this period in RCMP history, many members were strongly influenced by the Masonic Lodge, which permeated all levels of the organization.

LET NO MAN PUT ASUNDER

Just before I left Willmore detachment, my replacement arrived. He was a young member who had experienced a rather rocky start to his career in a nearby detachment. His arrival was preceded by warnings from his previous NCO, yet it was obvious our new member was determined to get off to a good start at Willmore. It is the customary duty of junior members to perform any necessary prisoner escorts. While performing one such escort, he managed to arrive in Edmonton safely and discharge his prisoner at the guardroom. As he made his way back to the detachment, he stopped to use the restroom, a major undertaking because of the uniform, equipment and regalia worn by RCMP members of that era. First, the Sam Browne belt with cross strap, lanyard and revolver were removed, along with the snug brown tunic. Then suspenders were doffed and breeches lowered. Much of the gear had to be hung on hooks or strung over the walls of the restroom stall. When re-robing, it was critical that everything be returned to its proper place. Our constable reassembled himself and returned to the police vehicle for the 100-mile drive home.

Later that evening, the city detachment received a report of two inebriated men staggering down the travelled portion of Highway No. 16, just west of the city. The two felons were, curiously, locked together with a set of RCMP handcuffs. They were taken to local cells and the handcuffs retrieved. The following day a police broadcast was issued asking members to account for their personal handcuffs. When the owner was not located that way, the authorities used the serial number to trace the cuffs to our recently arrived stalwart. An immediate enquiry was commenced to determine how the member's handcuffs ended up on the wrists of the two men. Evidently, the young member had a habit of carrying his cuffs draped over his Sam Browne belt. When disrobing at the service station, he had placed them on the toilet paper dispenser in the stall and neglected to return them to his belt. When the two men arrived a short time later, they found the cuffs. The rest is history. Sadly, this was almost the "culminating incident" for the member. He was charged in orderly room, which is the term for an internal RCMP disciplinary hearing for improper care of police equipment. His penalty was not severe, but the incident added to the weight of his doubtful performance record.

It surprised me to learn that the Masonic members of the RCMP had devised a drill team within their Alberta lodges. The team appeared in Masonic rites wearing the red serge of the RCMP, adorned by Masonic aprons and regalia. When I learned of the practice, I thought it was a blatant contravention of RCMP regulations and orders concerning the wearing of the uniform and sent an overt message to Masons indicating partiality and even fealty on the part of the RCMP to their lodge.

Filled with naïve, righteous indignation, I submitted a memo through channels to my officer commanding, respectfully requesting that the practice be ceased. I received an immediate response from the subdivision NCO on behalf of the OC. He relayed the OC's compliments and told me that my memo had been destroyed. I was also told that should I pursue my query regarding Masonry and the RCMP, I would quickly find myself walking down the road without a job, kicking horse turds and counting culverts. I learned that the OC, the subdivision NCO and a large majority of detachment commanders were all members of the Masonic Lodge. The matter was sacrosanct, and I had stepped far beyond the acceptable boundaries of a lowly constable. Any discussion about RCMP members allying themselves and consorting with a specific segment of the population was verboten. It was also never to be mentioned that being a member of the Masonic Order within the RCMP opened doors to opportunity and promotion.

Perhaps it is not surprising that individuals who were attracted to the Force also were drawn in by Masonry. Both organizations are secretive, steeped in tradition and bathed in rituals. Like the Masons, the RCMP is a charismatic institution. In fact, many of us would have enlisted and worked for no salary, just to be a part of this magical band of redcoats. The Force was very aware of this love of service and no doubt exploited it. Few members joined the RCMP just to better their financial situation. Employment in many government departments at the time was poorly paid, and the Force was no exception. It was widely known and understood that Canada's scarlet guardians worked ungodly hours for a pittance. Merchants in small communities frequently gave us discounts, lodges and clubs often waived membership fees for RCMP and local farmers could be seen dropping off meat and produce at the homes of detachment members. In spite of the minimal wages, taking any kind of additional employment was tantamount to treason. Members rarely violated this regulation; they knew that they could be dismissed if they were caught doing so.

As an additional burden—and this is still often true today—RCMP members were often unable to enjoy the festive periods in the year with their families. Christmas, Easter and Thanksgiving brought additional problems and the need for extra police staffing. Summer holidays were often postponed since the highways were glutted with the travelling public, again requiring additional law-enforcement personnel.

The Force demanded other personal sacrifices of its members. Marriage had been viewed as a nagging inconvenience to the early Force, and there were strict rules against it. Early in the 20th century, members were required to have seven years' seniority and the financial wherewithal before being allowed to wed. Those applying for permission to marry, however, were reminded that marriage was a privilege, not a right. Young RCMP members tolerated this unreasonable restriction as a price to be paid for serving in the legendary Force. The rules were relaxed to five years in the late '30s and two years in the late '50s. One also needed to have $1,200 in cash or convertible assets. It was obvious that the RCMP's senior management much preferred a complement of single men who could be moved at will a good deal more economically than someone with a wife, children and all the material effects and obligations that a family brings.

The organizational attitude toward members and interracial courtships revealed undercurrents of racism. Dating and engaging in social relationships with non-whites were discouraged, and members doing so were subject to punitive transfers. As matrimony was not permitted without permission, the Force scrutinized potential wives carefully.

Any request of marriage to a non-white wife was greeted with great discomfort and most likely denied. There are many examples of serving members who resigned so they could marry the woman of their choice. White Anglo-Saxon Protestants and Catholics governed the country, and many Canadian customs and laws reflected this dominance. When the great transition toward racial equality began in the 1970s, many senior members became extremely uncomfortable with what they perceived as the breakdown of long-established regulations in the RCMP. Again, the Force became a microcosm of change in the entire country.

Transfers were often used as a means of extracting members from what was judged a compromising situation. A young man getting in too thick with a local woman considered "not appropriate" would suddenly find himself transferred to another detachment. These decisions were made arbitrarily by detachment commanders, section NCOs and officers commanding. There was no room for negotiation.

Even if they didn't engage in unsanctioned relationships, few members served longer than three years in a community. It has long been debated whether it is more advantageous for members to become knowledgeable, participating members of a community or to distance themselves in a quest for objectivity. In my era, becoming too close to the community was reason enough to be moved on. However, this approach has changed for two reasons: first, there is less money for transfers than there used to be, and second, it is now seen as beneficial for members to become immersed in local activities. Police–community relations are very much in vogue, and members are encouraged to interact with all segments of the community. Recruits arriving at their first posting now can remain there for years and may not relocate until they receive their first promotion 10 or 12 years later.

CHAPTER 6

PRAIRIE ROOTS

In the summer of 1965, I moved to my next posting in the company of my new wife. Valley Bluff was located in northeastern Alberta. A typical western Canadian prairie community, it was primarily inhabited by people of Ukrainian background. Although the area's population was approximately the same as Willmore's, the detachment complement was somewhat larger. There were no town police, so the RCMP had the additional responsibility of policing the town of Valley Bluff.

I had admired the members of the highway patrol working out of my former detachment, so when I indicated an interest in traffic enforcement, I was assigned to the Valley Bluff highway patrol. Upon arrival I met the detachment commander, a highly respected sergeant, along with the highway patrol corporal, who I later discovered leaned toward eccentricity. Corporal Kip Rollins, a former pilot with the RCMP Air Division, had been caught taking an unauthorized flight with an RCMP aircraft into US air space. He was stripped of his wings and reassigned to traffic enforcement. Functioning under Kip's supervision was akin to sitting in on a poker game. One seldom knew what shift Kip himself was working or what his subordinates were expected to do. It was a classic example of a laissez-faire operation.

This former sky jockey seldom wasted time on niceties or stood on ceremony. One frigid winter day, a fatal motor vehicle accident occurred on a highway just east of town. Because of extensive damage to the vehicle, the dead driver could not be extricated. Kip ordered a tarp to be placed over the body to protect it from the unmerciful wind and cold; he then instructed the tow truck to remove the wreck. While the tow truck was en route to town, the tarp fell away from the corpse, exposing the body. As the twisted vehicle followed along behind the tow truck, the body was in full view lurching around inside the damaged vehicle. Understandably, horrified local citizens complained to RCMP headquarters. Corporal Rollins, never long out of hot water, spent a good deal of time unsuccessfully justifying his actions to management. There were few dull moments with this NCO at the helm. He moved on not many months after my arrival and was replaced, to my delight, by Corporal Gerry Tetzloff, the former highway patrol NCO from my first detachment, whom I deeply respected.

The mid-'60s was the muscle-car era in North America, and the "big three" manufacturers were competing to determine who could squeeze the most horsepower under the hood of the sportiest vehicle. It was particularly frustrating for the RCMP, which was loath to spend the extra dollars to equip police cars with more powerful engines. The young dependants of prosperous farmers in and around the community were buying Barracudas, Mustangs, Pontiac Grand Prix and Camaros. Returning home from jobs and universities on weekends, they terrorized the streets and highways. These rambunctious drivers virtually ignored the highway patrol, knowing they could simply accelerate away from an underpowered pursuing police car. Finally, in the late 1960s, the Force acquired high-performance vehicles that surpassed almost anything else on the road. We received our first hot rod police car with great satisfaction. Tucking in behind speeding muscle cars, we would swiftly overtake them and activate our emergency lights. The offenders would put the pedal to the metal, expecting to pull away, and were shocked when they realized their nights of wild freedom on the roads were a thing of the past. Now that they knew they could no longer outrun the police, high-speed pursuits became less common and a large measure of tranquility was restored to local streets.

Police work brought many lessons in tragedy and irony. On long weekends, we deployed extensive radar operations at strategic locations. It was not unusual to issue over 100 speeding citations during an eight-hour shift. On a typical long-weekend evening, the radar operation was set up on Highway No. 16, the busy east/west provincial highway. Corporal Tetzloff operated the radar unit while two of us occupied the interceptor car and stopped offending vehicles. After an exhausting eight-hour stint, we pointed out to Corporal Tetzloff that our hands and pens were wearing out. He finally relented, congratulating us on again writing over 100 citations. We dismantled our operation, feeling we had made a contribution toward reducing carnage on the highway. As we relaxed in the corporal's residence sipping coffee and enjoying the satisfaction of a job well done, we received an urgent call about a serious accident just east of town. Arriving at the scene, we found two vehicles that had been involved in a head-on collision. Two young men were dead in one vehicle, and an entire family of seven perished in the other. No alcohol was involved, and it was suspected the young male driver of one of the cars had fallen asleep and veered into the path of the other vehicle. The irony became evident when we discovered the accident scene was no more than 100 yards from our recently concluded radar operation.

Another fatal accident brought an interesting visitor to the community. In the early '60s, Japanese cars were a rarity on Canadian highways. The driver of an unusual car called a Toyota was travelling at a high rate of speed and apparently fell asleep and wandered off the highway. The car flipped end over end, coming to rest on its wheels. The body of the driver was found lying on the highway in front of the car. It was a mystery how he got there, as the windshield of the vehicle was intact. The traffic analyst surmised that as the car flipped several times, the driver was ejected out of the now-broken rear window precisely as the vehicle catapulted end over end. There were severe injuries to the victim's face and head. The closest next of kin available to identify the body was none other than Sergeant Bill Thorne, one of the most feared and disliked physical instructors in the RCMP training division. Many of us had memories of Thorne positioned on a large scaffold in the RCMP gym, grinding recruits through their paces. The more intense the training session became, the more he enjoyed inflicting anguish. He was perhaps a legend in his own mind, but many decades of recruits resented him.

When Thorne arrived in our community, we were surprised by his humility. Completely absent were the arrogance, sarcasm and cruel comments. Curiously, this instructor had never served in the field, and he appeared to observe in wonder the varied and difficult situations that confronted us. It was obvious his reason for visiting was intimidating him, especially when he encountered our mortician. As I escorted Sergeant Thorne to the funeral home, he looked like he was about to face the gallows. He was extremely pale and unsteady on his feet, and appeared nauseous. Although the mortician was often compassionate and caring, full of sympathy for the bereaved, his demeanour with the police was much more pragmatic. When Sergeant Thorne arrived at the viewing room and the sheet was pulled back to reveal his deceased nephew, Thorne blanched, turned abruptly and rushed out, stating that it was not his relative. It took some encouragement to persuade him to return and have a closer look. The mortician explained that most of the facial bones had been broken. While Thorne looked on, the mortician attached a pair of forceps to the deceased's nose and pulled. There was a squishing noise, and the face of the deceased took shape. The former terror of the gym shrieked out his positive identification and ran from the room. To soothe Thorne's jangled nerves, we took him out for a beer to help him regain his composure. He spoke to his former students in wonder, repeatedly saying he could never do their job.

Two significant events occurred while I was posted at Valley Bluff. In December of 1965 our son, Liam, was born, and in 1966 I attained my five-year anniversary with the Force. To recognize the five-year milestone, the RCMP awards a single star, to be worn proudly on the upper left arm, designating a journeyman policeman. A five-year member is perceived as an authority figure by those with fewer years of service, and management considers him capable of serving in positions of leadership. There was minimal celebration of the star, but it gave me great satisfaction to receive this badge of accomplishment.

During this era, there were regular occasions for great celebration and camaraderie within the RCMP. In the spring and fall, promotion lists were released across the country. Potential recipients would await these notifications with bated breath. Many would provision the liquor cabinet, anticipating hosting a promotion party. On the day the lists were publicized, members travelled to the nearest detachments, where impromptu celebrations materialized. These events would vary depending upon the magnanimity of the promotee. Some would be frugal, whereas others spent hundreds of hard-earned dollars on lavish parties.

Another annual event that brought the membership together was the rifle and revolver competitions. All RCMP members had to compete in qualifications to maintain their proficiency with issued weapons at operational levels. A central location was designated for annual shoots. Candidates travelled in groups of four via police transport to what was most often a bona fide weapons range. Although a serious endeavour, all personnel delighted in gathering for the day to see old friends and catch up with news within the Force. Every division and subdivision headquarters housed at least one former or wannabe drill instructor holding the title of discipline NCO. Among his many duties was conducting the annual shooting qualifications. While much socializing and tomfoolery would occur after hours, the actual protocol on the shooting line was strictly observed and enforced by the range master. Members who attained a score designating them as marksmen would receive further badges of prestige featuring crossed rifles and revolvers. These badges of excellence were hotly pursued, and those who earned them were granted the right to wear them for the following year.

Rural detachments like Valley Bluff were just beginning to receive secretarial services. Up until the late 1960s, members were expected to do their own typing and filing. One surprising day, we were introduced to Elaine Pasoula, 19, fresh out of secretarial school and our first detachment stenographer. Our bastion of maleness was ill-prepared for the presence of a woman. The first priority was cleaning up the colourful language commonly used in the office. The detachment commander introduced a cuss box to which miscreants contributed a fine, and it regularly filled to capacity.

At first, no one was prepared to surrender his carefully assembled thoughts to some woman who knew nothing about police work. Elaine, initially timid, shy and inexperienced, sat unoccupied, witnessing members busy themselves at their typewriters. Finally, disgusted with our intransigence, she sauntered over to a member busily committing the details of his investigation to print, tore the paper from the roller of the typewriter and demanded to be put to work. Quite taken aback at her pluck, the member ceded his seat at the typewriter and watched, transfixed. From that moment on, Elaine began inexorably to take control of the office. Soon we were squabbling over her availability. She was an amazing asset to the operation, quickly learning the mystique of crime reporting and organizing our paperwork as never before. Within a year, it was difficult to tell who ran the entire operation—the sergeant or Elaine.

During my early years in the Force, general duty personnel routinely logged 300 hours per month. Municipal and traffic units worked fewer hours. Detachment or district members worked a regular day shift conducting investigations but had to respond to all calls after hours.

MUSKRAT RAMBLE

Bob Connell was the owner-operator of a Valley Bluff auto body shop with a tow truck service. He was well known to the detachment, partly because he and his tow truck were a common presence at accident scenes and partly because he did all of the custom work on our cars, repairing any that were damaged, applying police decals to doors and generally keeping our fleet in good condition. Bob was a Second World War air force veteran who had flown bombing missions over Germany in a Lancaster aircraft. Highly respected for his wisdom and integrity, members frequented his business socially as well as professionally.

Although Bob's operation was thriving, it was anything but neat and tidy. He often came in late in the morning, wading through reams of invoices and assorted paperwork that lay strewn about his congested little office. One cool, bright spring morning, one of his staff discovered a muskrat in a culvert near the premises. He captured it and placed it in a cardboard box. I had arrived at the shop in advance of Bob and was met by the chap with the muskrat. He was unsure how to dispose of the creature, and it was obviously getting angrier and angrier in its confined state. I suggested that we address the package as though it had just arrived via courier to the auto body shop and set it on Bob's already cluttered desk. Soon after, Bob arrived to commence his daily tasks, one of which was to open newly arrived mail and auto parts. As he rubbed the sleep from his bleary eyes, Bob spotted the box and remarked that these must be the parts he was waiting for to finish a job. As we stood by, he removed the tape from the box and reached inside. Suddenly, a very angry muskrat, all teeth and claws, jumped straight out of the box. The rodent landed on the floor and scurried out of the premises, glancing back and giving us a final snarl. Bob fixed me with a baleful look, reached for a large wrench and came toward me. Seeing this, and knowing that discretion was much the better choice over valour, I too made a hasty exit. Even though I was attired in full uniform, complete with breeches and boots, I ran for my life down the street with the large, enraged, wrench-wielding man in hot pursuit.

It was not a good morning for the image of the RCMP. It took some time and talk and an offer of free coffee to bring Bob down to a rational state. Eventually he came to see the humour in the stunt, and the story lived on in legend for many years.

Senior management and detachment commanders considered manpower to be a limitless resource, and there was no requirement to curtail hours. Special events, such as country dances, rodeos, exhibitions and public performances constantly required additional policing. Members were assigned to assist communities hosting these occasions for as long as necessary; meanwhile, those remaining at the detachment worked double shifts for the absentees. Time off and annual leave were deemed to be privileges, not rights, and were granted only when they would cause no inconvenience to the organization.

Even though we always had to listen for the telephone, there was time to get to know some of the community members. Father Gordon Graham, a young local priest, observed a number of fallen-away Catholics within the detachment and decided to bring these sinners back to the fold. Attending our social functions, he became friends with several members. As the months passed, it became obvious the young priest was enjoying our lifestyle to the fullest. We learned later in 1966 that Gordon had left the priesthood and found a girlfriend, and was considering marriage. His replacement, Father James Toner, a young man with world-class musical talent, also decided he would embark on saving wayward mounted policemen. Father Jim learned to appreciate the anonymity and confidentiality of our convivial happy hours. Entering our informal lounge, he would pull off his clerical collar and reach for a beer. Father Jim provided valuable support to a member who had been traumatized by the failure of his marriage and even contemplated suicide. This caring priest intervened with empathy, understanding and positive counselling and probably saved the man's life.

Several of our group were musically inclined and gathered from time to time for an off-duty jam session at the local Legion. Our very musical cleric would join in occasionally. The local parish priest did not encourage Father Jim's rapport with community members, youth and the constabulary. He upbraided his understudy for ungodly musical appearances at the local watering hole and largely ignored the positive relationships the young priest had established. Once again, the crusade embarked upon by this second man of the cloth became diverted, as he too departed the priesthood, married and became a professional musician.

After a year on traffic, I transferred to general duty. I preferred the diversification of detachment investigations and was pleased to return to that line of work. Our highly respected detachment commander had moved on and unfortunately was replaced by another individual with a serious alcohol problem. The operation functioned in spite of him. Each night Sergeant Walker would retire to his quarters on the second floor of the detachment, crawling inside a bottle of whisky and becoming incapable of making any decisions. Luckily, Walker was seldom seen after 5:00 p.m. During detachment social functions, he would habitually drink to excess. He utilized these occasions to single out one or more of us for verbal abuse. Even though Walker was the senior man on post, he was largely ignored due to his minimal credibility. In spite of his incompetence, the code of silence among the members prevailed, and Walker's alcoholism was never divulged to senior management.

I was given the responsibility for policing Mustard, a village just east of Valley Bluff. For years, the small community had been intimidated by the members of one family. One set of brothers had inflicted their cruelty upon the populace and moved on, but now the second generation was coming of age. We were aware of the family's reputation, and it was part of my mandate to ensure that the locals were living with a measure of tranquility, not fear. Not long after my new responsibilities were assigned, I learned that one member of this clan in his early 20s was approaching seniors on the street and demanding money. He uttered veiled threats that included arson if people did not cooperate. Many of the village's older citizens were immigrants who harboured historic fears of police and authority figures; they did not see complaining to the police as an option.

One evening, along with another member, I conducted a patrol in Mustard. We had just checked a vehicle and were standing on the road when we heard the roar of an engine coming at us on the darkened street. As the car bore down on us, headlights out, we leapt aside, narrowly avoiding being run over. We ran to our car and gave pursuit with emergency lights on. We chased the car in and around town until it failed to negotiate a turn and ran into a ditch. Inside the car were three young men, and we found that one of them was the low-life who had been threatening seniors. Two of them surrendered, but the ringleader resisted. Perhaps he was trying to impress his friends, but he did not anticipate the wrath of those he had attempted to run down. He resisted and had to be aggressively arrested for dangerous driving, and all three men were taken to detachment cells. The ringleader continued to be arrogant and defiant, but was warned to stop intimidating the community. He appeared before a Justice of the Peace on several charges the following morning and was released on bail.

During this period, I was working with a junior member. Several nights after the Mustard arrests, he was parked in the village observing traffic. The recently released individual, again in the company of his gang, approached the lone policeman and threatened him, giving him an ultimatum to get out of his town. My junior partner called me about the predicament via police radio. I immediately drove to the village, talked to my partner and located the suspect at his residence. It quickly became obvious he had forgotten the conditions laid out for him a few days earlier. I arrested him for threatening a peace officer and violating his bail conditions. Because he was still resisting and defiant, I had to knock him to the ground and handcuff him before taking him once again to detachment cells. The following day, I was contacted by his lawyer, John Koshuta, who alleged his client had been brutalized. I knew and respected Koshuta, so I felt confident I could be candid with him. I explained how difficult this individual had been, justifying my use of force, and told him of the intimidation and harassment of senior citizens, the attempt to run us down and the threatening behaviour toward the constable. When court was convened, Mr. Koshuta pled his client guilty to assaulting a peace officer and dangerous driving. A lengthy jail sentence was imposed, and the offender did not return to the community on his release. We received many expressions of appreciation and votes of confidence from Mustard's citizens, who were relieved that the scourge had been removed.

Unfortunately, other lesser miscreants continued to plague Mustard. A local gang was committing a chain of break, enter and thefts. Although we knew who was responsible, acquiring sufficient evidence to support arrests and charges was a challenge. On a morning following yet another invasion of a local business, we knew some kind of intervention on our part was necessary. Glancing up at a large poster of a fingerprint in the detachment office, I was seized with an idea. I met with fellow investigators and we decided who among the suspected gang was the most vulnerable. We immediately picked up our target and brought him in for questioning. We let him stew for an hour or so, then I suddenly burst into the interview room with the large fingerprint poster. I asked him if he was prepared to talk, informing him that this was his fingerprint and it was found on the glass display case of the business that had been broken into. He remained mute for some moments, finally explaining that my accusation was impossible. When asked why, he blurted that he had been driving the getaway car and had never entered the building. His face turned white when he realized what he had confessed to. Omerta—the code of silence—had been broken. He eventually gave a full statement that implicated his accomplices. They were subsequently rounded up and charged with over a dozen break and enters that had occurred over several months. Five young criminals were convicted and sentenced to jail terms.

BIZARRE ACTS OF deviant behaviour can occur in any setting, including northern Alberta, but they are always astounding and shocking. The wife of a local farmer called us after finding three strange packages in the bottom of her deep freeze. When we arrived at the farm, we found three human fetuses or newborns frozen solid, wrapped up like chickens. The woman related that her 30-year-old daughter lived in nearby Edmonton and often visited the farm. Upon being contacted and interviewed, the daughter broke down and admitted that she had given birth on three separate occasions in her city residence, unbeknownst to anyone. She had become pregnant three times by different unknown men. A large girl, and rather slow mentally, her pregnancies might very well have gone unnoticed. She did not know how to care for the children and was unsure if any of the babies were alive when they were born, but autopsies indicated at least one of the babies had been born alive. She admitted to putting each one in her mother's freezer. While it was clear we had grounds to lay one murder or manslaughter charge, our discussions with the prosecutor produced a consensus that there was little value in using the full weight of the law against the accused. She had suffered enough through these tragic events. She was charged with three counts of disrespecting a human body and received a suspended sentence with a recommendation for counselling.

The case exemplified the type of human misery that can have a severe and lasting psychological impact on law enforcement officials. Even now, years into retirement, a dream will descend upon me and I will awaken in a cold sweat. The details will be vague, but I will recall enough to be reminded of a traumatic murder, a fatal motor vehicle accident or a suicide scene from my past. Recounting the incidents in this book has released memories that I thought were locked away forever. As I recall one, another suddenly follows, almost physically jolting me. It has been astounding to discover what I had hidden away, and I'm sure this is true for most former police officers.

Another strange and disturbing case occurred in Valley Bluff in 1967. An entire family—a husband, wife and three school-age children—had gone missing from their nearby farm. There were absolutely no clues as to what had happened to them. Relatives were contacted, police agencies alerted and bank accounts examined, but there was still no sign of the family. A small pond on the farm was dragged in case something had happened in the water. Months passed with no news or developments, and relatives were pressuring the police to do more. As the disappearance had created much stress and angst in the community, countless hours were dedicated to the file, yet no clues surfaced.

Then a neighbour reported seeing the father in the farmyard as the sun was setting. An immediate patrol was made and all buildings were searched, still without success. Although a police service dog had been involved earlier in the search, it was again called to the scene. The dog scoured the property, eventually leading its handler to what appeared to be a root cellar, locked from the inside. When the cellar door was pried open, we saw the missing family, dirty, gaunt and frightened, huddling together in the darkness. It was obvious the father was not pleased to see us. When asked for an explanation, his response was rambling and disjointed. He reported that the end of the world was near, and he had commanded his family to take refuge in the cellar; he went out at night alone to forage for food. They would ride out the end in this hole in the ground, armed with nothing but a bible. It was obvious he was in a detached mental state and had lost touch with reality. He had placed his family in considerable jeopardy, yet they were too intimidated to challenge him. They were all taken to hospital for examination and treatment, and the father was placed in a mental institution, where he remained.

While serving at Valley Bluff, I observed a classic example of good investigative work. The initial complaint involved what appeared to be an intentional poisoning. A bitter rivalry had developed between two men from Mustard. After drinking coffee in a local restaurant, one of the men became violently ill and was rushed to the hospital, where they discovered strychnine in his system. The detachment was alerted, and investigators traced the activities of the stricken man from the time he became ill. They examined a sugar bowl in the restaurant and determined it had been laced with poison. The victim's rival had been seen in the café on the date the poisoning took place.

During the course of investigator George Apps's enquiries, he learned the wife of the alleged poisoner had died under suspicious circumstances several years before, and her death had been attributed to a heart attack. Constable Apps realized he was on to something and began to research the wife's death. He learned that on the day she died, the wife had seen her husband off to work in the morning. Her routine was to accompany him outside, where she closed the garage door as he left. Then she returned to the house and had a cup of coffee with sugar. The deceased's mother happened to be at the house that morning and had been with her daughter when she died. When she described the manner of her daughter's passing, it appeared to have all the earmarks of strychnine poisoning. With this information in hand, Apps applied for a permit to exhume the wife's body in order to conduct an autopsy, which had not been done at the time of her death. Constable Apps subsequently visited the husband, who pumped gas at a local service station. He confronted the suspect, explaining that not only was he being investigated for the poisoning of his associate, but his wife's body was being disinterred for further tests.

At about three o'clock the following morning, which happened to be New Year's Day, news arrived at the detachment that the suspect had been found dead at his residence. He had thrown a large party to commemorate the new year and retired late in the evening. The cause of death was strychnine poisoning. The results of his wife's autopsy confirmed that she had also been poisoned with strychnine.

Not all duties were as interesting or challenging as a murder investigation. One of the many and varied duties foisted upon RCMP members is acting as agents for the provincial public trustee. In cases of sudden death where there are no apparent survivors of the deceased, RCMP members must take inventory of all items found in the victim's possession. It is often an onerous task, as many elderly people living alone tend to eccentricity and some are hoarders who have not taken care of themselves or their property. In one such case, we removed the body of an elderly man who had died in his shack, surrounded by boxes filled with his possessions. I knew the job was going to be challenging, so we began to separate items of some value from those that had to be destroyed. It was going to take days of painstaking work to clear everything away.

On about the third day, I was starting to deal with the kitchen area, which was laden with packages of unopened foodstuffs. Just prior to throwing a large tin of flour onto the garbage heap, I opened it and sifted my fingers through the flour. I will never know why I did this, but my fingers felt something solid in the flour. I pulled out a tobacco tin that had been concealed there. Opening it, I was shocked to discover that it contained $2,500 in cash. I immediately called for another member to witness my discovery and filed an exhibit report about the money. My find generated a human-interest story in the local paper, which included the deceased man's name. Subsequently, a living relative and his wife appeared on the scene to claim the money. At that point a good news story turned rather ugly. The great-grandson of the decedent alleged that the old man had been hiding money for years and that there should have been much more, implying that the police had found a larger stash and kept it for themselves. There was no basis for their claim, and we were exonerated.

Valley Bluff contributed many building blocks to my development as a peace officer. It was a stable community with a strong agricultural base. My work was complex and varied, offering many opportunities to practise the craft of law enforcement. Partway through my tour of duty, I was assigned to court detail. During the time I served at Valley Bluff, the member handling court detail performed all the duties of a modern Crown Counsel. Today, Crown Counsel manages court proceedings, including the approval of all charges. Formerly, the police decided on the appropriate charge, except in the most serious offences, when the Crown would be consulted. Although the current system better reflects the fundamentals of jurisprudence, I found that I learned a great deal through determining appropriate charges, handling a court docket, prosecuting less serious cases and even conducting preliminary hearings. It gave me confidence to express my point of view and is perhaps one of the reasons I was eventually identified for the training division as an instructor.

Our provincial magistrate, Orest Melnyk, was a retired farmer. His knowledge of the law was limited to his on-the-job reading, and his daily contact with members of the bar. The processing of the weekly court docket illustrated the close relationship the police enjoyed with the judiciary, which gave RCMP members a position of elevated community responsibility. In those halcyon years of the 1960s the police were allowed liberties that would be unheard of today.

Each week, prior to opening court, Magistrate Melnyk and I relaxed over a cup of coffee and went through each of the police files. We discussed each set of circumstances, and the magistrate "consulted" me regarding the penalty in the event of a guilty plea. A considerable amount of tact was required on my part, but if the individual was a repeat offender or was uncooperative at the time of the offence, I suggested that those factors be considered. Often the magistrate asked me to suggest an appropriate fine. In some cases of repeat offenders, I thought a jail sentence was appropriate. In each case, the penalty suggested by me or other RCMP members was followed to the letter. This approach worked to the advantage of the justice system and was quite equitable, as long as the police handling the court docket were not vindictive. However, it's easy to recognize the pitfalls of such procedures, which have long since been stopped, particularly with the demise of lay magistrates. In accordance with the timeworn adage "Not only must Justice be done; it must also be seen to be done," it became necessary to remove the police from such an intimate relationship with the judiciary. In the contemporary judicial system in Canada, the responsibilities of Crown, defence and police are clearly delineated.

Back then, the neutrality of the justice system was occasionally sorely tried. In one such case, an accused person appeared before a lay magistrate in a court close to Mountain Park. When this hapless chap entered a plea of "not guilty," the magistrate roared, "'Not guilty'? What do you mean 'not guilty'? The RCMP would not have brought you before me if you weren't guilty!'"

In those earlier days of prairie justice, it was not unusual for defence counsel to nurture the prosecuting constable, prompting him if he had forgotten potentially vital components of his case. The constable would quickly include the missing component, which might very well win the case for him. Such was the positive relationship between police and many solicitors.

DURING THE 1960S, in response to impaired driving and the resulting highway carnage, the Borkenstein Breathalyzer was invented to analyze breath samples to measure the amount of alcohol in the blood. I was interviewed to determine my interest in becoming a Breathalyzer technician/operator. Realizing this qualification could stream me back into traffic enforcement, I approached the opportunity with some hesitation. The Breathalyzer, however, was cutting-edge technology, and I wished to be involved. I returned to Regina for training, which was extremely rigorous. After successfully completing the course, I returned to my detachment, but not for long. In the winter of 1968, I relocated to Rostad, Alberta.

CHAPTER 7

DO AS I SAY, NOT AS I DO

The Breathalyzer operator in Rostad, which was located northeast of Valley Bluff, had been working alone and under considerable stress thanks to the demands of the new technology, so I had been sent there to give him some relief. When I arrived, however, my counterpart was transferred to another location. As the sole Breathalyzer operator, I was on 24/7 stand-by, in addition to my traffic responsibilities, which entailed alternating day and afternoon shifts.

During my first year at Rostad, I administered 300 breath tests. Life became a treadmill. Many of these breath tests were administered while I was on my regular shift. During the other 16 hours of my day, impaired drivers kept appearing and calls for my assistance did not stop. I simply sat at home and waited for the phone to ring. Because the Breathalyzer was new technology, many impaired driving charges supported by breath evidence were appealed to district court, compelling my evidential presence. The legal profession was challenging every aspect of the new impaired-driving legislation, thereby establishing court precedents through case law. While it was exciting to be involved in an initiative that would change community attitudes toward drinking and driving, it was also a time of inordinate physical and mental demands. Another operator came on board during my second year at Rostad, bringing some relief. At the same time, I was transferred to municipal duties.

Our second child, Michelle, was born in April 1968. This brought additional worry and stress, as she suffered from Rh disease and needed three blood transfusions shortly after birth. Because the local facilities were inadequate, she had been born in an Edmonton hospital and had to stay there until she was healthy enough to be brought home.

While the Breathalyzer duties were now shared, work on the town detail was equally demanding. Rostad was populated by francophones, English and Irish and was situated next to one of the largest Cree reservations in western Canada. The town detail consisted of a corporal and two constables, leaving only one person on the evening shift. The two hotel beer parlours were the source of many disturbance calls, especially on welfare and family-allowance payment days. Alcohol abuse was rampant, and the constable on duty, particularly during the evening hours, was solely responsible for preserving the peace and tranquility of the town.

In this occasionally unruly community, I witnessed the disruptive power of a woman. I will call her Agnes Stone. While her name is not important, her physical prowess most certainly was. Standing five feet four inches tall and almost as wide, she possessed a great capacity for alcohol but became extremely anti-social when drinking. If she was spotted under the influence, RCMP members would cross the street rather than initiate a confrontation. Much like the wolverine in the wilderness, it was in everybody's interest to avoid crossing her path. When she was in town, the entire detachment was on edge, secretly hoping she would quietly take on her load of liquor and pass out peacefully in a state of alcoholic bliss. Occasionally, she would find fault with something or someone, and the dreaded call requesting an intervention would arrive at the detachment.

On one of her more memorable junkets, Agnes created a disturbance at a local hotel. We knew more than one police officer would be required, so straws were drawn, and three stalwart guardians embarked to preserve the peace. We confronted Stone, respectfully asking if she had any interest in joining us in the police vehicle. She responded by throwing a chair at one of the members. Eventually, three sweating, torn and forlorn defenders of the peace returned to the detachment with our guest. When asked to vacate the police car, Stone promptly kicked out the back window. Sergeant Page, himself a large, intimidating presence, heard the disturbance and appeared on the scene to demonstrate how to deal with intoxicated persons. Assuming that our client would respect his rank, Page leaned into the back door of the police car to demand the lady's exit. As he placed his head in the car, she hit him with a Mike Tyson right jab on the side of the jaw, knocking him senseless to the pavement. Thirty minutes, several torn uniform shirts, one broken pair of glasses and very little dignity left among five exhausted RCMP members later, Stone was safely ensconced in a detachment cell. We could only hope this lady would someday marry and become enthralled with domestic life.

Rostad was my first exposure to a large Native community. At the time, communication between the detachment members and Native people was dismal, and encounters between the two groups were often accompanied by conflict. The predominant RCMP mindset toward Aboriginals was antipathy. It was not uncommon to witness aggression and occasional brutality in the cellblock. When a social gathering or dance was scheduled on the reserve, tension would build at the detachment. No proactive measures were initiated to reduce the possibility of trouble, but the police contingent was always highly visible at the event. Resentment and distrust were rampant between the factions, setting the stage for confrontation. Inevitably, police vehicles sustained damage, and from time to time members were injured. The response of many Native communities during this period of emerging militancy was predictable. Canada's federal police force was not welcome on their home turf and some Native youths viewed the RCMP as an "army of occupation."

COMPLIMENTARY TRANSPORTATION FROM THE QUEEN ⸻

There are occasional examples of individuals in the Force who resemble Joe Btfsplk from the old *Li'l Abner* comic strip, a chap who went through life with a visible black cloud over his head. There was one such member in Rostad. Never was there anyone who worked harder or tried more diligently to uphold the law than Rod Bowman. But more often than not, he would find himself rubbing up against some regulation or policy. One frigid winter evening, he was conducting property checks. It was 3:00 a.m. and ⁻30°F. To carry out these security duties thoroughly, members would routinely park and lock the police vehicle, leaving it running. This meant we needed to carry two sets of keys. On this night, the town was virtually dead with not a soul stirring. Constable Bowman had forgotten his spare set of keys, but as it seemed there wasn't anyone up and around, he left the police car running and unattended while he walked the back lanes. Returning to retrieve his car, he found nothing but tire tracks in the snow. In a panic, Bowman woke up his corporal, who alerted the sergeant. Several members were also roused, and an immediate search began, with all police personnel in the province being advised via police radio.

The following day, we received a call from the Cree reserve some 16 miles west of town. Apparently, there was an abandoned police car in the ditch on the reserve. The car was immediately recovered, apparently undamaged. No amount of probing revealed the culprit. It was assumed that, as was often the case, one or more of the residents of the reserve had become stranded in town after the bars had closed. The idling, unlocked police car must have been too much of a temptation. As could be expected, Constable Bowman found himself in service court charged with failure to safeguard RCMP equipment. He would be forever remembered as "the guy who lost his police car."

I was assigned to the district in my third and final year at Rostad. At the time, general duty personnel or detachment men were similar to general practitioners in the medical profession. We were responsible for all police activity in the rural area surrounding the community. We worked day shifts, conducting many diverse investigations, but were also on call at night. The large Native reserve fell within our responsibilities, and after-hours calls were numerous. A routine month would see most detachment personnel logging 14- to 16-hour days.

After responding to several of these after-hours calls and occasionally working well into the early morning, I took it upon myself to approach Sergeant Page with what I thought was a reasonable request. Knowing I was confronting a traditional leader who managed through intimidation, I approached his office with no small measure of trepidation. During my audience, I explained the problem of working late into the night and having to be on duty first thing in the morning. I suggested the option of allowing the member responding to after-hours calls to sleep later and commence his day shift at 10:00 a.m. Sergeant Page reacted in a rage, saying I had no business telling him how to run his detachment. I was upbraided for what he considered as insubordination. Page informed me that detachment members responded to any and all calls, and their lack of sleep was of no concern to him. He reminded me that he was required to operate in this fashion when he was a constable, and nothing was going to change. I was instructed to continue my duties and leave the running of the operation to him. If I was unhappy with this, I was welcome to request a transfer. It was another example of top-down supervision. Any suggestions from sub ordinates were more likely than not viewed as the start of insurrection.

My specific area of responsibility was the Cree reserve. I was required to train a new recruit but was largely left to my own devices. My first objective was to establish some rapport on the reserve. I contacted a tribal constable, Gerry Wuttunee, who had been recently hired by the band, and offered to coach him on criminal law and federal and provincial statutes. Gerry and I developed a good working relationship. One evening, I dropped in to the detachment while off duty and saw Constable Wuttunee in the public foyer, sitting alone as duty personnel were in the lounge having coffee. When I invited him into the lounge for coffee, he seemed somewhat uncomfortable but followed me into the room. We immediately encountered a cool silence, and two members got up and left. Later, when I asked them what the problem was, they told me there was no way they were going to drink coffee with an Indian. There were obviously some inherent bad attitudes within the detachment that would be difficult to change, and I realized the atmosphere was not going to get much better.

During this period, a senior constable name Wilf Cott received a promotion and transferred to Boulder, a small community nearby that bordered another large Native reserve noted for its plethora of social problems and alcohol abuse. Boulder was a small command consisting of a corporal and two constables, and it occurred to me that if any location needed an NCO with empathy, insight and a flair for innovative policing, Boulder was it. Knowing Cott's history, I was certain he was not the man for the job. He had spent several years at Rostad, a community fraught with problems identical to those he was about to confront. Cott was a surly, bitter individual who solved problems with physical force. Woe to the prisoner in the guardroom who hesitated to do his instant bidding! Cott tended to take his frustration out on Native clients in the cellblock, punishing individuals who were already almost defenceless thanks to excessive drinking.

Not long after Cott was settled in his new detachment, he received a call at his residence from a local gas station about a group of aboriginal men who had just departed the premises without paying for their fuel. The now Corporal Cott responded in civilian clothing and a marked police car. It wasn't long before he spotted the offending vehicle travelling on an isolated road on the reserve. Cott pulled in behind it with lights flashing. The vehicle stopped, and several young men disembarked. Carrying a shotgun, Cott confronted the driver. Without warning, he clubbed the young man with the butt of the shotgun. The other three men jumped Cott, knocked him down and viciously assaulted him. As he lay on the ground, barely conscious, one of the men picked up the shotgun and held it to the corporal's head. He was about to pull the trigger when one of the other occupants of the vehicle intervened. The man holding the shotgun had recognized Cott as the policeman despised by many Native people who had suffered at his hands. However, sanity prevailed and, after taking Cott's wallet and shotgun, the culprits left him on the side of the road, badly injured. Cott was later discovered by a passerby and rushed to the hospital.

This series of events precipitated one of the largest manhunts in the area. Dozens of policemen converged on the reserve in an effort to apprehend the suspects. After several days, they were caught hiding in a dwelling and surrendered without incident. All were charged initially with attempted murder. While Cott's unsavoury reputation did not give the young men licence to beat him so severely, many people in the community understood the history between the victim and the four accused, and it was widely anticipated that the defence counsel would bring up Corporal Cott's reputation during the trial. Whatever the reason, the charges were reduced to assault of a peace officer. The accused entered guilty pleas and were given lengthy jail sentences.

One would assume that a victim of such a life-threatening experience would pause and contemplate why it had happened. This was not to be. For years after the incident, the corporal would proudly display large framed photographs of his ruined face taken shortly after his admission to hospital. He wore his scars like badges of courage and changed nothing in his approach to policing. He retired soon after, having done much damage to RCMP relationships with Native people.

Back in Rostad, Sergeant Page's social behaviour indicated serious alcohol problems. On more than one occasion, while returning from an afternoon of drinking, he lost control of his police car, slid off a snowy road and landed in a ditch. He could be heard over the police radio calling for assistance, his slurred speech indicating his condition. Page had chosen two or three cronies at the detachment as his regular drinking pals. One evening, he travelled out into the district to locate two of these members who been drinking while on duty. Urgent calls had gone out to them with no response. Sergeant Page left the comfort of his home to search for them, found them and returned to the detachment. He took the two offenders into his office, closed the door and could be heard laying down the law. I could also hear his subordinates challenging him, advising that if any official discipline were to be meted out, they would be apprising management of Page's own indiscretions. Page capitulated and declined to pursue the matter. From that moment on, his credibility was tainted and his control of the operation diminished. As happened with many other unfit members, he would go on to be promoted unjustifiably.

AFTER SERVING THREE western Canadian communities, I had reached some conclusions regarding policing, demographics, the human condition and the state of my beloved Force. In all of these communities, most anti-social behaviour was carried out by approximately 10 percent of the population. This was true of white and non-white citizens. By virtue of their ethnicity, Native clientele were more visible, and police interaction with them was more conspicuous. It was clear to me that the social problems on most Native reserves were attributable to poverty rather than race. Inevitably, poorer people of all stripes tend to receive the most police attention, even though alcoholism and drug abuse are equally prevalent in affluent settings. The upper strata of the community do not generally attract police scrutiny, primarily because the abuse is subverted and less visible. When offences are discovered, the rich have competent legal teams to defend them in court. This is much less likely to be the case with those at the lower end of the economic hierarchy. Youth transgressions also receive greater police attention due to their higher visibility. A group of teens is much more likely to be challenged and charged with liquor and drug offences than their parents, who might well be breaking the same laws, but in a more private fashion.

I also observed that the prominent personalities in every town

I served, though they differed in gender, age and background, were strikingly similar from location to location in their self-image, attitude and demeanour. This was true not only of the town mayors but of others occupying positions of leadership in a community—town secretary, doctor, parish priest, car dealer or owner of the grocery store. In addition, not unlike physicians, police are privy to all the deep, dark secrets of the community, and therefore it has always been incumbent on them to use the utmost discretion. In small communities, the RCMP are very aware of who has alcohol or drug problems, who is abusing his or her spouse and who is cheating on whom at all levels of society.

In areas of the country where there are high concentrations of Slavic peoples, it was disconcerting to observe a clear and present irrational fear of the RCMP. This was especially evident among the elders who had emigrated from their native lands. Many of them were extremely nervous and even distraught when we would arrive at their farms unannounced. Some would hide in an attempt to avoid contact. As I got to know some of the older people personally, I queried them on their seeming initial discomfort with the police. It seemed the uniform we were so proud of—the forage hat, breeches and boots and distinctive brown tunic—projected an image not dissimilar to that of the German storm troopers and Gestapo who so terrified certain Slavic nations that were conquered and occupied during the Second World War. It was just another example of how skewed perceptions can be. When we learned of this surprising reaction, we took extra care to reassure those who needed reassurance that we were indeed there to serve, not persecute.

Surprisingly, high-profile crimes such as murders and serious assaults were often the easiest to solve. Most violent offences are committed by someone known to the victim. This meant we were often able to make quick arrests and then spent most of our time on the case preparing for court. The primary law-enforcement focus at that point was ensuring evidence was properly collected and catalogued. Every effort was made to consider the rights of the accused. Members learned these procedures thoroughly during their service and often received additional support from specialized sections when a serious crime was committed. By far the most energy on a typical general-duty police operation was devoted to preservation of the peace, protection of property and incidents pertaining to motor vehicles. These routine incidents filled our days and sometimes became monotonous. Only occasionally were we titillated by more serious offences. It was always interesting to witness the enthusiasm and dynamism with which members embarked upon a major or unique investigation.

Perhaps the most attractive aspect of general-duty policing was the diversity. Even though much of the work was mundane, the phone often would ring and send us off in an unexpected direction. Occasionally, while conducting enquiries, we would come across information that would either open a new investigation or surface leads to a current one. Unlike working at a factory job or in a bank, no two days were ever the same. Perhaps the key to this was the uniqueness of the citizens and their different reactions to the police.

By 1970 I had nine years' service and was at the low point of my career. The detachment work environment at Rostad was toxic. Morale was low, and I wanted out. In some ways it was paradoxical, as my time at this detachment had been a vast learning experience due to the complexity and volume of police work I had encountered. There was an astounding diversity in investigations, and this had been the most demanding and intense of my work assignments so far. Sadly, it had also demonstrated—yet again—how a detachment should not be managed.

The inherent flaws in RCMP management practices demonstrated by detachment commanders were very disturbing. The expectation of unrealistic work hours and lack of recognition was demoralizing. There was nowhere to turn to voice dissatisfaction. Occasionally a staffing officer or NCO would visit to interview members, but no complaints were uttered and none were expected. In the unlikely event that a member expressed a concern about his detachment, he was instantly put on the defensive and told it would be far better to settle differences locally rather than air them outside the detachment. The cavalry regiment mentality was pervasive. All decisions were for the "good of the Force," and this attitude was consistent across the country. Precisely when I was contemplating resigning from the Force, I received a call from my section NCO. He had been asked to identify potential instructors for the training division in Regina and wished to submit my name as a candidate. That phone call would change my career and perhaps my life.

All RCMP members carry memories of their training experience, not all of them pleasant. Consequently, I had misgivings. A corporal whom I respected in a neighbouring detachment was a former instructor, and I sought his input. He advised me not to turn down this opportunity, as it was one of the peak experiences in his own career, so I immediately informed the staff sergeant of my interest. Soon after, I was sent on a month-long odyssey consisting of an instructional technique course in Ottawa, followed by a course for potential instructors in Regina.

At the Canadian Police College (CPC) in Ottawa, candidates learned the basic tools of adult education. The courses were taught by skilled instructors and enhanced my confidence amazingly, especially when speaking in front of a group. Yet the experience was not without stress, as there was a pass/fail component and some candidates were unsuccessful. After completing the two-week school of instructional technique, we travelled to Depot Division in Regina, where we were presented with the opportunity to ply our new teaching skills. We were closely scrutinized by the experienced instructors, who had a vested interest in determining our suitability to join their faculty. Soon after my return from Regina and Ottawa, I found out that I would be posted to the academic section, Depot Division.

CHAPTER 8

FLAILING AT WINDMILLS

Upon arrival at the training division, I was reassured to see that the sadistic and torturous methodology of the old-time instructors had fallen out of favour. Radical changes were taking place in the training curriculum and in the Force itself. The hours once devoted to equitation were now freed up for more relevant and contemporary topics. More time was allotted to academic subjects such as criminal law, federal statutes and practical training. The introduction of female recruits loomed as an additional engine of change. Training for new instructors included teaching through the establishment of learning objectives, giving the program much-needed structure. The study of human relations was in its infancy, but Corporal Dal Langenberger, the NCO in charge, was attempting to re-mould the former "cavalry curriculum" of PT, foot drill, riding and harassment, which aimed to "break" the candidates. Another welcome addition was the presence of French-language counsellors to assist unilingual francophone recruits.

In spite of the changes, high expectations prevailed. The Depot training experience was still stressful for recruits. We were starkly reminded of this when a young man took his own life. The timing of the incident was especially disturbing, as his troop had just completed their entire program and celebrated their ceremonial pass-out ceremony. The following day, as troop members prepared to embark to their respective postings, they returned from the midday meal to find their comrade lying dead in their dormitory with a self-inflicted gunshot wound, his issue service revolver at his side. His family, who had been on hand to share the elation of his graduation, had not yet departed and had to be notified. He left no note to explain his state of mind at the time. It remained a total mystery why he had killed himself at the culmination of his lifelong dream. The tragedy put a pall upon the training division for some time.

As the saying goes, you don't have much opportunity to contemplate your options when you are up to your ass in alligators. That is the fundamental plight of every law-enforcement officer. He or she is constantly dealing with the ugly underbelly of humanity. It is impossible not to be cynical when witnessing the depravity of mankind on an almost daily basis. Working at the training division was like finding an oasis in the morass of human misery. I benefitted from ordinary working hours with weekends off, and the academic environment gave me the opportunity to question, read, debate and analyze. There were opportunities to discuss hypothetical scenarios and dissect real-life situations that went wrong. It was a priceless opportunity at a most critical period in my service.

During my initial year at the training division, I taught typing, report writing and practical training, which exposed recruits to simulated police situations. My second year was dedicated to teaching criminal law. Finally, I was assigned to the federal statute unit, an area I was quite unfamiliar with. I was fortunate to be working with Corporal Langenberger, an innovator whose influence would endure for the rest of my career. In addition to federal statutes, he proposed a block of training dedicated to human relations. One would expect this type of training to be offered in a police-training curriculum, since law enforcement is almost entirely concerned with human behaviour.

A SERGEANT MAJOR NEVER FORGETS

Music has always been part of my life. During basic training I became involved with the recruit bugle band. There was little else about me that would warrant the attention of the sergeant major, the man who ruled Depot. Sergeant Major MacRae owned the drill square and struck terror and awe in the hearts of all creatures daring to encroach on his sacred ground. He strutted like a peacock and roared like a lion.

One crisp winter's day, just before Christmas of 1961, Sergeant Major MacRae summoned me to his lair in the administrative block of Depot Division. As I stood at rigid attention, he instructed me to assemble a small quartet of brass musicians from the recruit population. On Christmas Eve, we would go around the square under the streetlights and play Christmas carols to the homes bordering the square. His final instructions were that under no circumstances would we sub-humans (recruits) enter any of the said residences. Even if an invitation was extended, we were to decline, play our yuletide music and return to barracks immediately after our mission.

Christmas Eve arrived under a blanket of subarctic air. The temperature was ⁻30°F, so we had to soak our instrument valves in alcohol to keep them operational. Alcohol, incidentally, was not to be used to warm the cockles of our valueless hearts. Off we trundled, bundled up in several layers of sweaters beneath our pea jackets. Things were going well in spite of the cold evening. As we stood under the streetlights and played our carols, residence lights flashed on and off in appreciation.

As we assembled beside the home of Inspector Mortimer, a newly commissioned officer, he opened the front door and invited us in out of the cold. I respectfully declined, informing him of restrictions from the sergeant major. He responded by saying that it was Christmas Eve and 30 below, and promptly ordered us into the house. The home was full of guests. We were led into the living room in front of a roaring fireplace. After playing some carols, we initially declined but eventually gratefully consumed some eggnog. It was a wonderful respite, and we rewarded the occupants by breaking into some Dixieland numbers. After a period of revelry, we bade our adieus and continued on around the square, our playing much inspired by the demon rum.

At the end of the following training day, I received a curt message to report to the sergeant major. I headed to his office, hoping for some praise about our carolling the previous night. As I approached the man I feared most on this globe and saw the thundercloud on his brow, I sensed impending doom. While I stood rigidly at attention, Sergeant Major MacRae, not in a gentle voice, asked if I recalled his final order the day before. Before I could answer, he emphatically reminded me of his explicit instruction not to enter any Depot residence while on our carol patrol. My explanation that we were under orders from a commissioned officer only brought more abuse down on my poor trembling shoulders. Rather than receiving kudos for a job well done, I was told in a most colourful manner that any future I might have had in the force was in severe jeopardy. The conversation was abruptly concluded, and I was summarily dismissed. I relayed the sergeant major's compliments to my cohorts, and together we considered our futures with some trepidation.

Ten short years later, I had the good fortune to be transferred to Depot as an academic instructor. In spite of the carolling incident, I had always had the greatest awe and respect for Sergeant Major MacRae. One of the highlights of my return to Depot was meeting him again, as he was now Inspector MacRae and the division training officer. As new instructors, we were invited to the administration building to have morning coffee and meet this legendary denizen of Depot, this time as subordinates, not recruits.

As a large number of us gathered, we heard the sound of his boots clicking down the hall. He appeared, resplendent in dress blue tunic, breeches and boots. A large stogie extended from his luxurious handlebar mustache. He looked as fearsome as Attila the Hun. We all stood at attention as he entered the room. He glanced over the crowd, and his eyes came to rest on me. I felt flattered that he would single me out among my peers. Then, in his booming baritone and with a twinkle in his eye, he said, "I thought I told you to stay the Hell out of the officers' houses!" He then wheeled smartly and left. My amazed co-workers demanded to know how I could have offended the training officer so quickly. I told them it was too long a story.

Bill MacRae still chuckles when I remind him of the incident. One of my lifelong heroes, this revered and charismatic man is now in his 80s. We remain friends to this day, though even these many years later it is discomfiting to address him as "Bill," for he will ever be "Sir." His complexity and contrasts as a man, and his many and varied legacies to the RCMP Academy are lasting treasures.

However, the traditionalists of the training academy took exception to anything smacking of psychology. They resisted vocally whenever an opportunity presented itself—on the worksite, in the coffee room or in the Corporal's Mess. Fortunately, Corporal Langenberger had the ear and support of both the chief academic instructor and Inspector MacRae, the training officer.

Corporal Langenberger proposed an introductory salvo of 18 hours of basic psychological theory enhanced by role playing that addressed domestic crisis intervention, one of law enforcement's most deadly types of interactions. He invited actors from the local professional actors' guild to play quarrelling couples whose arguments escalated to a potentially violent level. The recruits watched the actors and witnessed the escalating circumstances as spectators. At the moment when the police might be called to intercede, random pairs of recruits were chosen to enact an intervention, applying the skills they had learned in the classroom. Initially, the methodology was trial and error, and both the actors and the fledgling policemen made mistakes, but as the scenarios evolved the settings became more realistic. Recruits gained valuable knowledge and made their errors during training rather than in real life. The experience had a great impact on the students; in critiquing their Depot experience, they marked domestic crisis intervention training as the most relevant and significant information they had learned. When recruits who had been trained in this area went out to work in the field, their supervisors expressed amazement at their coolness and presence of mind when they encountered their first family quarrel.

Langenberger invited professors from the University of Regina to lecture blocks on psychology, sociology and perception. The recruits were exposed to opinions sometimes diametrically opposed to their own. Since they would contend with these divergent philosophies in everyday life as peace officers, it was essential that they gained this broader understanding. As time progressed, additional hours were found for sessions on policing minorities. Doctors Bruce Sealey and Neil MacDonald, amazing professors from the University of Manitoba, helped to revolutionize cross-cultural training and aboriginal policing across Canada. Dr. Ted Van Dyke, a cultural anthropologist, gained renown and credibility as a result of his work at Depot. He went on to become a foremost authority in his field.

Many questions that had plagued me as a result of my experiences with Native people were answered by these insightful people. I had always been mystified by the unwillingness of aboriginal people to want to change the behaviour of others. When problems were identified, whether it was a child's truancy or substance abuse by a relative or neighbour, no one in the community would tackle the problem head on. The professors taught me about the ethic of non-interference. In many aboriginal cultures, the concept of telling someone else to modify an attitude or behaviour is foreign. They believe that an individual makes choices and is the sole master of his or her destiny, almost from birth. This helped to explain the reaction of aboriginal parents when confronted with a child who refused to attend school. They would respond by telling authorities their child had been reminded to attend school, but the child had decided otherwise. This was deemed sufficient by parents, and they would go no further to discipline their dependant with respect to the decision not to abide by the rules. Parents in a white society would tend to force their will upon the child, but the ethic of non-interference precluded a Native parent from taking more stern action. It was imperative to recognize and understand such cultural differences.

As these professionals gained exposure at the basic training level, requests came from field personnel seeking more information. Dr. Van Dyke was contracted to conduct cross-cultural seminars to experienced policemen in Alberta. The sessions were held at a military base near Edmonton. As everyone assembled for the first day of the course, one policeman approached the professor, asking permission to speak to the group before the session commenced. He informed his classmates there would be a liquor run for those wishing to enjoy a libation at day's end. With that, the spokesman began to take orders, listing enough liquor to sink a battleship. With that task completed, the candidates took their seats, the lecturer was introduced and the session commenced. The course objectives were explained, and Dr. Van Dyke invited any and all questions. A seasoned veteran opened with, "Doctor, why do Indians drink so much?" The query seemed genuine, and the irony was apparently lost to all. It afforded Ted a natural opening to enlighten his students about the socialization of alcohol consumption. He explained that our prevailing North American culture is derived from societies that had been exposed to *spiritus fermenti* for thousands of years, and even so there are countless examples of addiction and abuse. The mainstream societal approach to consumption is very different from that of aboriginal peoples; when most non-Natives consume liquor, there is an attempt to disguise its effect. Everyone is familiar with the term "holding one's liquor." The more we can consume without demonstrating any effect, the more successful we are deemed to be. Aboriginal people's approach to the drug is perhaps more honest, and this may be partially attributable to their brief history with alcohol. When they feel intoxication, they succumb to it. There is no effort to conceal the effect, and uninhibited behaviour is witnessed. This, coupled with their higher visibility as minorities, makes them much more conspicuous. The discriminatory legislation that existed under the Indian Act, which prevented them from possessing or consuming alcohol, no doubt exacerbated the effect. These clear, logical and concise analytical explanations changed my perspectives toward aboriginal people and alcohol, and I saw others who were similarly affected that day.

Across the USA during this period, the FBI was experiencing violent confrontations with Native peoples, particularly on their reserve lands. As federal officers, FBI members were responsible for policing Indian territory. Dr. Van Dyke was invited to speak to them in an effort to alleviate serious widening rifts. His work in the USA, though initially greeted with cynicism, greatly improved Native–police relations and reduced conflict.

My understanding of the issues facing First Nations people, particularly Native youth, was also shaped by the novels of Canadian author W.P. Kinsella, which I discovered while at the training division. Kinsella's novels are tragicomedies about young people struggling to make sense of their lives as contemporary Natives. Although he is not Native himself, Kinsella bases his stories on his contact with First Nations youth who lived on the Hobbema reserve and frequented Wetaskiwin, Alberta. While it may sound frivolous, I learned more from Kinsella's fictional characters than from all the academics. The novels are told from the point of view of young Natives on the outside of white society and eloquently describe the sometimes poignant and sometimes hilarious dilemmas they confront. I learned much through the characters' attitudes and behaviour toward white society and gained empathy for the difficulties facing youth living on reserves and consequently on the edge of Canadian society.

Corporal Langenberger, who had taken university courses, suggested that I might consider doing so as well. His encouragement set me on the path to earning a bachelor of arts degree with majors in psychology and law. It was discouraging to watch Langenberger's peers resist his efforts to professionalize policing. They would berate him at work and even insult him at social functions when his wife was present. Opposing instructors voiced their opinions in class, discrediting the human-relations curriculum. But Langenberger was indomitable. He simply kept his shoulder to the wheel, making progress despite the hoots of derision from his peers.

SHOW US YOUR DELTOID

In the early '70s, the physical training staff at Depot were headed up by an enlightened senior NCO with a master's degree. He decided to augment the recruit's physical training experience with some basic knowledge of physiology. Accordingly, the recruits were given lectures in anatomy. Following their classroom sessions, recruits assembled in the gym at the commencement of their PT class. Instructors would call out a troop member's name and demand that he identify a bone or muscle on their person.

During this particular era, a young man named Bayman arrived from Newfoundland to begin his basic recruit training. From the outset, it was obvious that he was going to have some difficulty adjusting to the mystique and dogma of the RCMP Academy. One of the first indications of a problem arose when he encountered one of the drill instructors. As the young Bayman walked by the drill corporal, he acknowledged him with the folksy greeting, "How she goin', my son?" The corporal, after recovering from apoplexy, shook his drill baton and explained in no uncertain and very colourful terms how an NCO is to be addressed in a military setting, specifically by rabble such as a recruit. The islander took the discussion in stride. When he felt that the conversation was coming to a close, he departed with a "God luv ya." The corporal vowed that he would witness the youngster's demise if it were the last thing he did.

Word of the problem recruit quickly spread, as did his infamy. He continued to be unflappable and, to the chagrin of the instructors, unstoppable. In spite of being a very open target almost everywhere he went, our candidate from the east coast remained irrepressible and progressed quickly through the training experience. The instructors compared him to crabgrass. They just could not be rid of him.

Now I fast forward to the troop in the gym. Yes, it was his troop, during the first class after lunch in mid-July, and the gym was full of summer tourists. During the oral quiz in the gym, several anatomical areas had been correctly identified. Suddenly, the Maritimer's name rang out, and the instructor demanded, "Show us your deltoid." The recruit responded slowly and with apparent confusion. "I can't, Corporal," was the reply. Again the instructor roared out his name, "Show us your deltoid, you rabble!" In an instant, the recruit's shorts were down. His jock strap remained in place, but the gesture clearly indicated where he thought his deltoid was located. There was an instant furor in the gym as onlookers roared with laughter. Even the instructors supervising the troop lost their composure and could not contain their laughter.

Not long after this incident, the physiology classes seemed to fizzle. The Newfoundlander became the toast of Depot. He was known forever after as Deltoid. Interestingly, the recruit from round the bay graduated successfully and went on to serve in the Maritimes, where he became a highly respected detachment commander.

Inspector MacRae, respected and feared, learned of the conflict and met with the entire staff. He clearly outlined his position regarding human-relations training, stating that he was the one who had arranged for most of the university professors to lecture the recruits. He concluded by warning the entire instructional body that the next individual who offered unwarranted criticism of this program would be on his way out of the training division. The road became somewhat smoother following this meeting, but there was still an undercurrent of resentment. Years later, both Corporal Langenberger and then Superintendent MacRae would receive commissioner's commendations for their efforts, a reward for their far-sightedness and perseverance. Many of Langenberger's innovations still form the basis of human-relations and simulation training in the RCMP and police forces worldwide.

Many serving and former members shared an antipathy toward academia, and this was even evident within the Parsons family. One might expect that a father and son who worked in law enforcement for the same organization would have much in common. Such was not the case, particularly when I became involved in contemporary police training. My father's tenure in the RCMP spanned an era when the Force discouraged any outside interference and disparaged academics as theorists with their heads in the clouds. Native policing had always been paternalistic, and Aboriginals were treated like children. Inviting university professors to Depot Division to speak to recruits was akin to heresy, while efforts to understand First Nations culture were deemed a waste of time. Over the years, I learned to avoid topics such as this in my father's house, since our discussions would inevitably escalate into shouting matches. Even though my father was a compassionate policeman who always tried to do the right thing, like many of his peers he resisted change and felt threatened by the incursion of lay people into the sanctity of RCMP training.

The author dressed in the parade uniform of the Lord Strathcona's Horse (Royal Canadians) Regimental Band. Note the similarity to the RCMP uniform. The famous Sam Steele of the North West Mounted Police was the first commanding officer of this distinguished Canadian cavalry regiment.

The original Depot Division drum and bugle band. The author is on the extreme right of the top row. Terry David Mulligan, later a well-known TV and radio personality, is in the third row, third from the right, and Jim Treliving, founder and owner of Boston Pizza, is the drum major standing on the far left.

The graduation photgraph of "A" Troop, July 1961, prior to the new members' transfers to the field. The author is in the front row, second from the left.

Superintendent W.F. MacRae, corps sergeant major at the RCMP Academy in Regina while the author was a recruit, photographed in 1975. Superintendent MacRae was held in awe by all recruits. He "owned" the drill square, and indeed all of Depot Division, striking terror in the hearts of all who dared to encroach on his sacred ground. He strutted like a peacock and roared like a lion, yet in unguarded moments displayed the intellect and vocabulary of a university scholar. The complexities of his character and his many and varied legacies to the RCMP Academy are lasting treasures to all who served with him. MacRae's son Fraser also joined the force and became the officer in charge of the Surrey, BC, detachment, the largest in Canada. He retired with the rank of assistant commissioner. MacRae's second son, Graham, also served with distinction in the RCMP.

The author with RCMP detachment personnel in 1967; he is standing on the extreme right.

The father of the author, Superintendent Joseph Parsons (retired), presents the author with his 20-year service medal at Regina in 1981.

To Supt. Joseph Thomas Parsons (RTD),
formerly of
The Royal Canadian Mounted Police.

Supt. J. T. PARSONS (RTD)

This plaque commemorates fifty years of continuous police service to Canada by the Parsons family, September 1, 1930 to September 1, 1980

Reg #10851, Cst. Parsons, J.T. Engaged: Sept. 1, 1930 at Regina, Sask. Retired: Feb. 20, 1966 at Ottawa, Ontario.

S/Sgt. I. T. PARSONS

Reg #22033, Cst. Parsons, I.T. Engaged: July 3, 1961, presently serving at "Depot" Div., Regina, Sask.

Presented September 27, 1980 during Saskatchewan Homecoming Celebration of RCMP Veterans at Regina, Saskatchewan.

A plaque presented by the Parsons family to Superintendent Joseph Parsons commemorating his 50 years of continuous service to the RCMP.

The Academic Training Section, RCMP Depot Division, Regina, circa 1982. The author is sitting in the centre of the front row.

The author toward the conclusion of his RCMP service, Carman, Manitoba, August 1988.

MV *Catherine Pearl*, the author's private vessel that was used to make contact with various detachments along the coast of Vancouver Island.

The author presents his stepson, Constable A.W. Giesbrecht, with an RCMP badge in July 2008, while his proud mother, Lynne, observes.

Comox District Free Press

Profile

BEYOND POLICING

Retiring RCMP Insp. Ian Parsons a pioneer in community relations

RCMP Inspector Ian Parsons retires Monday after 33 years of service

Parsons: new recruit

And as a dashing-looking veteran Mountie

< Newspaper article regarding the author's retirement.

∨ Late in life, the author has returned to his first love—making music. During their teens, Danny Bereza and Ian Parsons honed their music skills as part of the iconic Northernairs dance band in Whitehorse. After they both completed satisfying careers, they reunited to form the duo Silk Pajamas, playing jazz standards, country, rock, blues and Latin music.

CHAPTER 9

CULTURAL IMMERSION AND SWEETGRASS

As the summer of 1973 arrived, it was time for me to rotate back to the field. I hoped to return to Alberta, a province I knew and loved, preferably to command my own detachment. I naïvely believed that I might have some influence over my transfer. I travelled to Division Headquarters in Edmonton with that purpose in mind and contacted division staffing branch members, who told me I had been pencilled in as the commander of a small detachment in a farming community. Returning to Regina, I anxiously awaited notice of my transfer. Some weeks later, my connections in Alberta conveyed their regrets, informing me that the commanding officer had amended my posting. He felt that NCOs returning from the training division should not be given their own detachment at the expense of those who had remained in Alberta coping with day-to-day police work. I was to be the new operations NCO at Blackfoot Crossing, Alberta, the second-largest Native reserve in the province and a location fraught with social and law-enforcement problems. Most RCMP members dreaded the possibility of working in this community.

As disappointed as I was, the policy of the commanding officer seemed fair. While in the training division, I had been espousing more effective methods of aboriginal policing. The opportunity was at hand to apply the theory. To my chagrin, the larger-than-life detachment commander at my new location had a reputation as a "clean-up" man. A legend throughout the land, he was a prepossessing figure who delighted in physical combat. I was fearful that this would not be a match made in heaven, as our philosophies were bound to clash.

Blackfoot Crossing was a town of 400 serving a reserve of 4,000. It was a ramshackle, run-down settlement with bars on all the businesses' windows. About the only thing that had never happened on Main Street was a gunfight—and that occurred while I was there. The RCMP building was one of the largest in town, with half of the structure comprising jail cells. As I entered for the first time, my perceived nemesis, Sergeant Lawrence "Larry" Sifton, towered over me and invited me into his office. He opened the conversation by describing serious problems on the reserve. Sergeant Sifton had also recently arrived, and he shared his intent to improve the health and welfare of residents rather than contribute to their miseries. As he outlined his ideas of personalized policing, I was reassured since they corresponded with everything I had hoped might be accomplished. We concluded our discussion, and Sergeant Sifton seemed very pleased, remarking that we had better get started.

Sergeant Sifton was the one of the most amazing people I would work with in the RCMP. He was extremely perceptive, very bright and completely knowledgeable about RCMP policy. There was never a bad day with this man. His one flaw, as I had so frequently encountered at previous detachments, was his fondness for alcohol. Even when drinking, he functioned at a high level, disguising any evidence of intoxication. His drinking was cyclic; as suddenly as he began, he would cease and not touch a drop for weeks. Although it never detracted from his duties, it was pervasive. Over time, it affected his marriage and other aspects of his life. He had the potential and the intellect to reach any level in a police organization, but the direction he chose no doubt imposed a ceiling on his upward mobility. He was a most unusual and charismatic human being, revered by the aboriginal people and loved by his men.

Armed with initiatives and objectives set by Sergeant Sifton, we began to develop our plan. In previous years, aggressive behaviour between reserve citizens and the detachment had been a problem, resulting in an unusually large number of charges laid of assaulting a peace officer, resisting arrest and obstruction of justice. The tribal police consisted of three members who worked closely with the detachment. We immediately established stronger ties with them through workshops on basic police procedures. Both the sergeant and I became members of the reserve recreation association. The sergeant founded a youth boxing club in which I assumed the role of fitness trainer. The club was an instant success with Native youth.

One of our young charges demonstrated great skill in the ring. Six feet tall and 18 years old, he was in prime condition. He was intimidating even when sparring, and few other youths were interested in engaging him in the "sweet science." Sergeant Sifton opted to act as a punching bag for our young Muhammad Ali. As they sparred, Sifton encouraged the young man to strike, which he did with enthusiasm, soundly delivering jabs and crosses to his coach. As the sparring progressed, and just when the blows seemed to be too much for Sifton, the young man suddenly found himself lying on the floor in a daze. The counterpunch delivered by the coach was never seen by the victim or the spectators. Those of us witnessing the session came away with a new respect for our boss. He not only was a skilled boxer, but he also actually enjoyed being hit. Could there be a more lethal combination? Following the sparring session, the young man seemed to have developed empathy for his opponents. He became more restrained when training with his counterparts and showed more interest in developing his technique than annihilating his fellow boxing students.

I COULDA BEEN A CONTENDER

Sergeant Larry Sifton, the legendary Blackfoot Crossing detachment commander, was renowned for his size and physical prowess. He was also highly respected for his sense of fairness and energetic non-enforcement involvement with the youth and the community in general. The tribal recreation association, of which both the detachment commander and I were members, hosted an annual provincial aboriginal youth boxing tournament. In his capacity as boxing coach, the sergeant became highly involved in organizing the event.

The commanding officer of the province and the officer commanding the subdivision were slated to be in attendance at the finals of the tournament, which provided additional impetus to ensure the success of the event. It occurred to me to that the reigning Canadian heavyweight champion, George Chuvalo, might be a real celebrity attraction at the tournament. He was available and indicated he would be pleased to attend.

Clifford Many Guns, chief constable of the tribal police, was also legendary among his people. In his earlier years, he had been a renowned rodeo bronc rider and a professional boxer. When he learned that Chuvalo would be at the tournament, Clifford could hardly contain his excitement. After the champ finally arrived, I noticed the chief furtively measuring up Chuvalo on several occasions. You could almost see the wheels turning. He seemed to be saying to himself, "I think I could take this guy."

During the final matches of the tournament, the recreation centre was filled with several hundred people, leaving standing room only. I was the ring announcer, and George Chuvalo, at ringside throughout the tournament, refereed some of the championship matches. Chief Many Guns was lurking on the periphery, obviously in awe of the Canadian heavyweight champion.

I seized the moment and announced that later in the evening we were in for a real treat. I told the audience that our own tribal police chief Clifford Many Guns had agreed to participate in a three-round exhibition match with the Canadian heavyweight champion. A great cheer emanated from the crowd. It was the first time I had ever witnessed a proud member of this tribal confederacy turn pure white. Clifford appeared to be having some kind of a seizure. I let the crowd hang for a moment, then announced that although the chief was willing to proceed, George Chuvalo had declined due to contractual issues. I then glanced over at Clifford and winked at him.

It was clear that Chief Many Guns was torn between his irritation with me for putting him on the spot and relief at not having to box the Canadian heavyweight champion. I guess he didn't really want to find out if he could stay in the ring with Chuvalo after all. He remarked to me some days later that he had no idea how imposing George Chuvalo was until he stood beside him. In the weeks and months to come, I paid a substantial price for my folly, as Clifford was extremely resourceful when it came to devising and carrying out practical jokes.

For the hours he devoted to training youth on the reserve and the many and varied initiatives for which he was responsible, Sergeant Sifton was inducted into the Blackfoot Nation, given a Native name and made an honorary chief. The prestigious ceremony took place during a provincial Native youth boxing tournament in the presence of the commanding officer of the province and the officer commanding of the subdivision.

In my capacity as operations NCO, I attended all band council meetings, briefing tribal leaders and responding to their concerns. We also participated in social functions on the reserve. The tribe hosted large powwows that included Native groups from across western Canada. These were considered sacred events, devoid of alcohol and filled with traditional dancing. An age-old gambling activity known as hand games had great significance and popularity. In addition to luck, these games required concentration and skill. We would often enter a police team, and the people took great pleasure in watching us participate in hand games. Occasionally, much to their surprise and ours, we would win.

As had been the custom for decades in this community, the provincial judge and his entourage travelled from Calgary to dispense justice. On their way they would habitually stop at the detachment for coffee and a social visit; then the judge and the police would arrive en masse at the modest courthouse. The judiciary and the police were either oblivious or unconcerned that this communicated an alliance or lack of impartiality, which in turn suggested the futility of challenging such power.

One of the relief magistrates was a retired commissioned officer of the RCMP. He was a pompous man who demanded that detachment members respond to him as though he were still an officer. When appearing in his court, police personnel had to wear their brown tunics, even at the peak of summer. In hot weather, the order of dress for detachment members was short-sleeved shirts with an open neck. In the interest of formality and at the expense of the comfort of RCMP members, the presiding judge demanded a tie and tunic in his court.

When I began to handle the weekly court docket, I suggested to Sergeant Sifton that we comply with our order of dress and dispense with the tunic. He agreed and encouraged me to appear in court in authorized summer dress. When I opened court, the judge appeared from his chambers, took one glance at my dress and ordered me to adjourn and see him in his chambers, where he informed me I was improperly dressed. I explained that Force policy dictated my current attire. He glared at me, stated that this was not the end of the matter and commanded me to reopen court. Because of his foul mood that morning, many were given jail time when they could not pay their fines instead of being granted more time to pay.

The good judge wasted no time in contacting Superintendent Peter Wright upon his return to Calgary. He was apparently shocked when my superior supported my decision to wear summer dress while attending court in 86°F weather. Later that summer, our new permanent magistrate appeared on the scene and took steps to ensure the perception of neutrality. He decreed he would not be stopping at the detachment prior to the opening of court. He took great care to remain impartial, and when an accused person appeared without counsel, he would often act as an advocate. It quickly became obvious to the population that there had been changes in the dispensing of justice. My mind wandered back to Valley Bluff and the days when Magistrate Orest Melnyk and I discussed sentencing prior to opening court. Much had changed in the administration of justice in a few short years.

ONE OF THE tribal police members was a victim in residential schools and carried deep psychological scars as a result. On more than one occasion, after a bout of drinking, he would utter threats against a local priest, a long-time resident of the community and former teacher. The priest had taught at the Indian mission school, which had closed after being tainted with scandal. To prevent a confrontation, we occasionally took the band constable into custody until he sobered up. He would make allegations of sexual abuse against the priest, then recant them, which made it difficult to investigate the matter with a view to laying charges.

The constable's trauma reflected the agony of a whole generation of Native people who had been psychologically, physically and often sexually abused by the residential school system and many of its teachers. Native children were taken from their homes, denied access to their language and culture and placed in boarding schools run by religious orders. The disastrous policy was perpetrated by church and state in apparent good faith for the betterment of Native people, but in hindsight it is clear the schools almost destroyed a culture and most assuredly demoralized it. The system created a generation of citizens with low self-esteem and many severe behavioural and personality problems. Combined with abject poverty, the residential schools devastated Native people across Canada.

Attitudes within the Blackfoot community changed noticeably as a result of our efforts. RCMP members caught the mood being set by the NCOs and became known on the reserve by their first names.

COMMUNITY RELATIONS

While stationed at Blackfoot Crossing as the operations NCO, I regularly met with the band council to discuss policing. Since we had established a good working relationship, one of the band leaders approached me in a confidential manner following a meeting, obviously wanting to discuss something. He intimated that, like many of us, every once in a while he had an urge to go on a bit of a toot. He did not wish to drive his vehicle after drinking and asked for some advice on what to do. I suggested the next time he decided to have a few drinks, he could bring his vehicle up to the detachment, leave the keys with me and I would take care of it. He was very appreciative, and I respected his forethought.

Some weeks later, we had a visit from our section NCO. He was in the detachment, examining our operation when a pickup truck driven in a rather erratic manner suddenly arrived in front of the building. A gentleman exited the vehicle and walked toward the detachment entrance. It was obvious he had been drinking. He asked for me, handed over the keys to the vehicle, tipped his hat at the staff sergeant and promptly left the detachment on foot.

The staff sergeant was aghast! He demanded an immediate explanation from me as to why the man had not been arrested for impaired driving. I described the arrangement I had with the citizen, observing that while his intentions were good, he had been a tad late in handing over his keys (and thinking to myself that his timing could not have been worse).

I assured my superior that I would be in touch with the band councillor to remind him of the importance of securing the vehicle before the party started. The section NCO, a pragmatic man, was not unfamiliar with the cultural setting. He understood that Natives did not necessarily interpret time in the same way we did. He looked at me askance, shook his head and mumbled something about how much less complicated police work was in "the good old days."

Native citizens began to see the detachment as a vital part of their community, perhaps for the first time in many years. The number of police–citizen confrontations resulting in criminal charges dropped dramatically, even though our detachment cellblock took in more prisoners than the Spy Hill provincial jail—2,400 in one year.

We experienced the conflict and crime characteristic of poverty-stricken communities, which meant our workload was demanding. High numbers of arrests occurred when extra money flowed into the community on welfare Wednesdays and when family-allowance payments were received. The detachment guardroom grew crowded while clients were being processed, and there was potential for chaos when intoxicated persons waited in line, jostling one another.

On one busy night, a particularly obstreperous woman who often caused problems when under the influence was confronting others aggressively while waiting her turn in the detachment cellblock. Constable Don Pittendreigh, who was known and respected on the reserve, bellowed out her name. All fell silent, and tension filled the room. Don approached the woman stealthily, telling her that if she caused any more trouble he would give her the biggest French kiss she ever had. The troublemaker beamed a large toothless smile at the constable, and a roar of laughter erupted. It was that kind of rapport that often saved the day when tensions were high.

Our good relationship with the people on the reserve also helped us to work with a young victim to stop a sexual predator. By some quirk of genetics, the men of the Lampson clan were of massive dimensions. They all stood over six foot three and weighed in at 300 pounds. We learned that over generations the Lampsons had been responsible for innumerable sexual assaults on women. Any woman was a potential target—married or single, old or young. On several occasions, the Lampsons' offences were disclosed to the RCMP and investigations were launched, but inevitably the victims, fearing reprisal from the Lampsons, recanted their story.

Late one evening while Constable Barry Hawryluk was on shift, 17-year-old Laverna McDonald appeared at the detachment. Her clothing was ripped, and she was in a very emotional state. She

CLAUSTROPHOBIA

The setting is one of Canada's largest First Nations reserves during the late '60s. A member of the RCMP detachment, who later earned the nickname Earthquake because of his massive physical size, received a call about a domestic disturbance. It was the middle of a very warm summer day, and he decided he would respond solo. Upon his arrival at the scene, he found two women—a mother and her daughter—in an intoxicated condition and causing a disturbance. Although he did not have a matron, he decided to take them into custody to prevent further calls. He removed them from the residence and placed them in the rear of the detachment paddy wagon.

On his way back to the detachment, he received and responded to another call. He dealt with it in a cursory manner and continued his return. As he travelled through an isolated section of the reserve, he thought he heard a clink of glass from the rear compartment where the ladies were being held. He stopped the vehicle and discovered that while he had been out of the truck, the two women had reached through the security screen and liberated some seized bottles of beer that had been secured in the front seat. Earthquake opened the rear door of the paddy wagon so he could restore order. To accomplish this, he had to squeeze into the secured portion of the vehicle. As he struggled with the two women, the rear door closed, locking him in with his charges and the beer.

Intoxicated by Lucky Lager and the presence of a virile constable, both women thought the situation ideal for a party and told the constable so. It took a good deal of poise, no doubt acquired in the training academy, for our stalwart guardian to regain and maintain control of the situation. As the police vehicle was in a remote area, several hours passed before it was found. It is unfortunate that a transcript of the discussion that took place inside the van was not recorded for posterity. Needless to say, Earthquake greeted his rescuers with a large measure of relief and gratitude.

It was said that from that day on, Earthquake was somewhat claustrophobic when inside any vehicle and would never sit in the rear seat of a police cruiser, which, of course, has no inside door handles.

disclosed that she had been raped multiple times by a drunken Lionel Lampson. Hawryluk made an immediate patrol of the reserve and discovered Lampson sleeping it off at his residence. Lionel was in his 30s and, true to his Lampson lineage, stood six foot four and weighed well over 300 pounds. Perhaps thanks to his inebriated condition, he dutifully accompanied Hawryluk back to the detachment.

At about 3:00 a.m. I was called to assist Constable Hawryluk. All of Lampson's clothing was removed, and he was given a set of coveralls to squeeze into. By this time he was sobering up and starting to realize the predicament he was in. He sat in a chair as I stood in front of him. We were almost eye to eye, even though he was seated and I was standing. Making sure that my corporal's chevrons were very visible to him, I told him that he was under arrest for the rape of Laverna McDonald. A flash of rage appeared in his face. I knew that if Lionel were to become violent, he would tear me, Barry and the detachment into little pieces. In a very firm voice, I demanded that he accompany me into the cells and warned him that any resistance would simply get him in more trouble than he was in already. He rose slowly from his chair and followed me into the cellblock. I closed the cell door firmly, looked at Barry and heaved a sigh of relief. We both knew that if things had gotten out of hand, the only way we could have stopped Lampson was to shoot him.

Even Sergeant Sifton was skeptical of our chances for a conviction. He assured me that if we were successful, he would buy us a bottle of whisky. Lampson was remanded in custody, and the trial date was set. Constable Hawryluk stayed in constant contact with Laverna McDonald, our witness and victim. He coached and counselled her, promising that we would protect her before and after the trial. She had misgivings but bravely persisted. At the trial, she gave excellent evidence, and Lampson was convicted and sentenced to four years in the penitentiary. For the first time in generations, the Lampsons knew they would be held responsible for any sexual assaults they committed on the reserve. Constable Hawryluk and I got our bottle of whisky.

Just when we felt police–community relations were moving in the right direction, Constable Zulak arrived. He was loud, arrogant and brash, openly disliked Native people and had just enough service that his little knowledge was a dangerous thing. Within a few short weeks, the slurs and comments he passed while working on the reserve led to an explosive situation. One sultry summer night, I received a troubling call at my residence indicating that two of our constables were being held hostage in the beverage room of the Corsair Hotel, 12 miles east of Blackfoot Crossing. Jumping into uniform, I headed to the Corsair. When I arrived, a number of people were standing outside the hotel in the street. I entered the beverage room and found it in total disarray. A number of patrons were lined up along one wall, and Constable Zulak and Constable Blanch, our recruit, were standing next to a table where two large young aboriginal men were seated. Zulak's shirt was partly ripped off, and he was in a state of rage. I told him to calm down and tried to get to the bottom of what had happened.

Apparently the two male patrons had been refused service because of their disruptive behaviour. When they refused to leave the hotel, Constable Zulak and his partner responded. The manager of the hotel, aware of Zulak's bad reputation, was worried when he entered the bar. Zulak approached the two men aggressively, informing them they were under arrest. The young men were slow to react, and Zulak, exhibiting his well-known impatience, loudly informed them that he would count to three and if they refused to leave, he would move them. After the count, Zulak grabbed one of the men and was thrown to the floor. The bar patrons then closed in on the two constables in a threatening manner and the standoff commenced.

I realized Zulak had made the situation much worse, both through his attitude and through his previous negative encounters. When I asked him to leave the bar, he hesitated, so I told him in no uncertain terms to "get his ass out of there," and he complied. It was at this point that the residual goodwill between reserve residents and the detachment began to pay off. I focused my attention on the two miscreants, telling them that they had committed several offences, including assaulting a peace officer, and they would have to accompany me. Thankfully, their attitude was almost apologetic. They told me that Zulak's arrogant attitude had made it impossible for them to cooperate with him, but they eventually accompanied me out of the bar, into the police car and back to the detachment where they were lodged in cells. They were eventually convicted for refusing to leave a licensed premise and causing a disturbance.

Zulak was counselled on his attitude, but it was obvious he was not going to change. He had never established any credibility among the people he was responsible for policing. Sergeant Sifton asked management to transfer Zulak elsewhere, but we were told we would have to continue working with him. We knew he was a flashpoint on the reserve and hesitated to assign him duties where he would cause trouble. We restricted him to office duties, and the other members had to shoulder the extra responsibilities. Over time, we did what one must often do in bureaucracies—we lied. Zulak also desired a transfer, and his ambition was to be a member of the highway patrol. We felt that was a perfect job for him. Sergeant Sifton submitted a report outlining Zulak's amazing transformation of attitude and the fact that he was desirous of traffic duties. Soon after, our "problem" was transferred.

During the era of Wounded Knee, around 1974, the militant American Indian Movement was active south of the Canadian border in North and South Dakota. Dissidents in many large Canadian reserves were also fomenting insurgency and rebellion. Some of the Native youth on our reserve had taken to wearing red head bands and gesturing with closed fists to communicate "red power." We had noted an increase in surliness in our day-to-day contact with young people. There was a general attitude of restlessness and even alienation.

One of our best constables, Don Pittendreigh, had accidentally run over and killed a sleeping Native man while patrolling through a wooded area adjacent to the town. Media headlines implied the RCMP had killed a helpless and aged Native man. A reporter from a daily newspaper in Calgary took it upon herself to pillory the constable's actions, using the incident to portray the RCMP in general and our detachment specifically as authoritative, uncaring brutes who harassed and persecuted Native people. Sergeant Sifton took exception to what he believed to be unfair reporting and contacted the journalist. He invited her to travel to our community and witness first-hand the quality of policing. She arrived to accompany patrolling constables for two nights. After her experience, she wrote a piece describing the positive relationships she witnessed between police and Native people. It seemed the most significant factor that altered her thinking was the amount of restraint exercised by RCMP members when under extreme duress. She interviewed many members of the community who expressed satisfaction with their local police, in spite of the tragic incident that had recently occurred.

An investigation into the accident took place, and the coroner ordered an inquest. On the day of the inquest, hordes of media and militant Native activists filled the town. Some members of the press were observed actually contributing to the emotionally charged atmosphere by covertly egging militants on to create some sort of disturbance. The coroner's jury, consisting of citizens from the reserve, determined the RCMP not criminally responsible. They recommended, however, that officers conduct walking patrols through the narrow, congested pathways rather than drive.

At the peak of intensity during the inquest, an urgent call came in reporting a serious motor vehicle accident on the outskirts of town. Along with the town's only fire truck and ambulance, I went immediately to the scene and saw two semi-trailer trucks had collided head on. One driver was dead and the other was still in the cab of the truck, which was on fire. The flames were so intense that it was impossible to reach the driver, who burned to death as we watched helplessly. The incident made an already emotionally charged day even more stressful. In the end, residents of the reserve refused to align themselves against the RCMP, maintaining that we provided a good service and were considered their police force. It no doubt worked in our favour that Constable Pittendreigh, the member who had accidentally killed the citizen, had entered a burning residence on the reserve several months earlier and rescued three children. The people knew this man had a good heart, and they extended their total support to him.

Sergeant Sifton's sense of fair play was once again evident during the investigation of a sudden death. The body of a young woman was found in a vacant residence on the reserve. The cause of death was difficult to determine, and the specialized general investigation section (GIS) from Calgary arrived to assist us. A young Native man with a lengthy criminal record had been recently paroled and was back on the reserve. When the GIS investigator became aware of his presence, the man was picked up for interrogation. The investigator was known for his aggressive tactics, and we heard him shouting while inside our interrogation room with the young man. Then came the sounds of furniture and bodies bouncing off the walls. It was obvious from the exchange that the investigator was demanding a confession. The young man denied any involvement, and there was no evidence to implicate him. When Sergeant Sifton heard the sounds of the fracas, he intervened. He removed the investigator from the interview room and privately informed him that his assaultive approach would not be tolerated. Aware of Sifton's potentially volatile reputation, the visiting detective immediately changed his bullying approach. Later it was determined the woman had died of natural causes. The suspect realized the sergeant had defended him, and word of his actions in support of the young man spread throughout the reserve, further reinforcing to the citizens that Sifton insisted on fairness, impartiality and respect.

The community policing initiatives carried out at this detachment and the positive results they generated became known throughout the province. Both the media and neighbouring detachments expressed interested in our methodology. We had proven that enhancing the police profile and presence with reserve residents reduced police–citizen confrontations and made the job of law enforcement safer. It was extremely satisfying to both Sergeant Sifton and me that we had brought positive change to a Native community through his experience and intuition combined with new concepts I had introduced.

Superintendent Peter Wright, officer commanding of Calgary subdivision, was a well-regarded, upwardly mobile executive, widely known for demanding high standards. He had a reputation as an intimidator and was known to be tough on detachments. When conducting a red serge inspection of a detachment to the west of us, Superintendent Wright discovered members with overlong hair and shabby kit and clothing and found the detachment in need of cleaning. Dismissing the members, he informed them he would be returning to re-inspect the following day. He left no doubt in their minds that he expected a vast improvement in all areas. When he returned to find the entire detachment spotless, the OC fired question after question dealing with difficult aspects of the criminal code. Many of the responses were incorrect, further irritating the superintendent. He again reprimanded the detachment commander, who realized he was in a no-win situation.

We learned our detachment was next in line for an inspection. As the member with the most recent exposure to the training division, I suggested to Sergeant Sifton that we practise some parade movements with our subordinates in anticipation of the arrival of "Himself." Some weeks later, upon the superintendent's arrival, the sergeant called the full complement of red-coated members to attention. He saluted, informing the OC the men were ready for inspection. He examined all the members, querying them on pertinent aspects of the criminal code. The men had turned themselves out well; acting on intelligence received from the previous detachment, they had studied the criminal code. After they had answered questions correctly, Superintendent Wright informed the sergeant that the men had passed muster. The sergeant asked for permission to break the men off. Somewhat puzzled, Wright assented. The sergeant immediately commanded in a loud voice, "Officer on parade, break off!" This compelled specific movements where the men came to attention, saluted, turned to the right smartly and marched off. The superintendent was so delighted he appeared on the brink of orgasm. The rest of the inspection went off without a hitch, and from that day on, we could do no wrong in the eyes of this uncompromising taskmaster.

It was just as well that Superintendent Wright never got wind of another, less successful initiative of mine. Two local men were suspected of bringing large quantities of drugs from Calgary to the reserve. Their trafficking activity was contributing to increased drug addiction and violent offences. Having lived in the city for several years, the pair had developed a certain level of sophistication when it came to avoiding detection, and we were finding it difficult to interrupt their lucrative business. I approached Sergeant Sifton with what I felt was an innovative idea. The subdivision general-investigation section had visited us recently on another matter and had left their very expensive voice-activated portable tape recorder behind. I wanted to plant the tape recorder in a cell. We would arrest the two suspects and hold them in cells for a limited time, hoping they might engage in an incriminating conversation. The sergeant was skeptical but willing to give it a try. After hiding the recorder, we arrested the two subjects and lodged them in cells. We waited anxiously, hoping we might get a break. Suddenly we heard swearing and loud smashing noises. Rushing into the cellblock, we discovered our charges had found the tape recorder and stomped it into smithereens. Bearing in mind that our tactics were somewhat questionable, it was going to be difficult to charge the pair with willful damage. We reluctantly released them and recovered what was once a $1,500 tape recorder. Needless to say, there were numerous memoranda exchanged regarding this incident. I realized then that I would not soon be considered a candidate for special operations.

I had completed several university courses while at the training division. As a result, I was listed as a candidate for a sergeant's position at headquarters in Ottawa. Once again, I struggled with the decision to leave the field and sought the counsel of subdivision management. I was told that there were many junior NCOs in the province who were senior to me, so the likelihood of promotion in the near future was remote. Sensing an opportunity, I accepted the Ottawa transfer. I was delighted when Sergeant Sifton informed me that the Native community wished to host my farewell party. Many citizens from the reserve were in attendance, and I was surprised and honoured when presented with a chief's ceremonial headdress. The posting that I had thought would be an unpleasant experience turned out to be one of my most rewarding.

By this point in my career, I had accumulated enough experience to make some further observations regarding the policeman's lot. First, no matter what the community's demographics or location, some segment of the population will want to test a new RCMP member. The challenges can come from someone in a position of power and influence or from the underbelly of society. Every member of the Force should be prepared to demonstrate that they cannot be bluffed or pushed around, whether they are in council chambers or on a dusty street. If a police officer doesn't understand that these encounters are real and inevitable, he or she can be compromised and ineffective.

Second, an unruly, aggressive woman is vastly more difficult to arrest than a man. This was even more of a problem when there were no female police personnel. Women can be as physically strong as men, and occasionally more vicious. Society demands restraint on the part of policemen when taking a female into custody. In every community, there is a female powder keg just waiting to explode. Members encountering women in such confrontations do so with great trepidation.

Police officers have been kicked, slugged, bitten and verbally abused by drunken or violent women. On occasion, retaliation must be physical, and the optics are almost always distasteful.

In addition to these important lessons, a much bigger issue became apparent to me during my time at Rostad and Blackfoot Crossing: the difficult relationship between the RCMP and aboriginal citizens in Canada. At one time, the police were viewed as a friend to First Nations. During the signing of Treaty #7 in southern Alberta in 1877, Chief Crowfoot of the Blackfoot Confederacy told his people, "The police have protected us as the feathers of the bird protect it from the frosts of winter." But over the following decades, this solid expectation of support and protection all but disappeared. The relationship between police and First Nations has occasionally polarized into animosity and even hatred. Canada's police forces had little input into creating the prejudicial legislation that governed Native people, yet police have always been tasked with enforcing cruel and discriminatory laws, including the unreasonable liquor provisions of the Indian Act. Under that act, an Indian "off the reserve" was forbidden to possess an intoxicant. To avoid prosecution, some Native people would drink as rapidly and quickly as possible. It is unlikely anyone would be socialized into drinking sensibly when faced with such conditions. In the recent past, before the more discriminatory sections of the act were repealed as a result of court challenges, police were even known to enter Native homes without warrant and seize any liquor they found.

These acts of oppression caused many First Nations people to have bitter memories of police. This was further exacerbated when police participated in the apprehension of children who were placed in mission schools to be deprived of their culture and language. Too often, these schools were the scene of horrific abuse, and children were left with vivid memories of police involvement in these traumatic events. The police are one of the primary agencies of the "white world" that First Nations interact with, but their opinion of police is seldom positive.

Local Mounties are often viewed with suspicion and only occasionally with begrudging respect.

A federal government study from 2008 reported that 22 percent of the federal inmate population in Canada is of aboriginal descent, a shamefully disproportionate figure considering that First Nations make up only 3 percent of the overall Canadian population. The figures reporting incarceration of aboriginal youth are equally disturbing. The abject poverty, isolation and anomie that afflict Canadian First Nations people are primary factors contributing to anti-social behaviour and alcohol and drug abuse. It is a disturbing issue for law-enforcement personnel, who do not have the tools, wherewithal or mandate to solve such vexing social problems. Yet police continue to be the "arm of power and authority" over those who have no way of escaping the morass of poverty and depression.

It is unsettling that a police force that historically set out to be friend and protector of our First Nations people has somehow become alienated from them. Many questions remain unanswered, even in the 21st century. What is the role of the police in Native law enforcement when, for years, governments have erred and are even now slow to resolve the plight of our First Nations? Should the police turn a blind eye to etiology? Should they ignore social inequities and dispense the law "Without Fear, Favour or Affection"? Such analysis and introspection is a difficult process that tends to place law enforcement on a slippery slope. Some will say this kind of deliberation is not the role of the police; however, I would argue that our craft has reached a level of professionalism that demands critical analysis of our actions in these often precarious social settings.

It is incumbent upon senior police administrators to be aware of social dynamics and ensure that first-line officers understand the reasons behind the problems experienced by the Native communities they serve. Police have historically been given the powerful option of discretion in enforcing laws in our country. This has always been an awesome responsibility. Political pressure is often exerted to direct enforcement to areas with high crime rates, often in less affluent neighbourhoods, and police strive to satisfy political masters yet maintain fairness and equity of enforcement at the same time. Police leaders have a responsibility to act as a buffer for first-line officers who may be exercising innovative enforcement options.

Providing policing service to an aboriginal community requires special skills acquired through additional education and in-service cross-cultural training. Above all, it is important to recruit and encourage members who have an interest in First Nations policing and who are aware of the difficult and disastrous path Native peoples have trod for the past two centuries. To ensure optimum staffing, consideration should be given to offering incentives for aboriginal policing duties, such as service pay and subsequent promotional opportunities. While laws still have to be enforced, and the incorrigible element will always be present, law-enforcement officers who demonstrate knowledge of community history and exhibit empathy and understanding will be viewed by Native citizens as part of the solution, not part of the problem. Recognition of cultural mores and elders has great worth, as does involvement in community events and sporting activities. The police gain respect, confrontations due to alienation are diminished and officers are safer. In addition, qualified aboriginal RCMP members should be identified and promoted in order to participate in the supervision and management of the organization.

Sadly, the difficult transition of our aboriginal peoples into mainstream Canadian society is ongoing. The complex socio-economic problems associated with First Nations communities will remain well into the 21st century. Canadian police need to be viewed as supporting this difficult transition rather than suppressing a people who have been unjustly treated.

CHAPTER 10

PUZZLE PALACE AND BEYOND

My first year as a researcher in the RCMP Planning Branch Headquarters, called the Puzzle Palace by many, brought a promotion to sergeant, a host of new experiences and a great deal of learning. During that era, Planning Branch was tasked with forecasting the needs of the Force across Canada and spanned all levels of policing. In January of 1975, I was assigned to a section that responded to various studies as directed by the commissioner's secretariat. I worked exclusively on a feasibility study on the implementation and ramifications of overtime, gathering and compiling data from across the dominion to assess the impact of paid overtime on the Force. This study gave impetus to one of the most dramatic changes in RCMP history.

The proposal to pay overtime met with initial resistance. I interviewed Superintendent R.H. Simmonds, then officer commanding of Vancouver subdivision, who would later become the commissioner of the RCMP. Simmonds disagreed with any form of overtime payment, remarking that paying overtime would compel him to identify and promote people who could manage resources rather than advancing those individuals who were competent policemen. It seemed that awareness of the two separate sets of skills was a new concept to him. Simmonds emerged from a generation who felt it unnecessary to reward hard work with money. After many interviews, I realized that traditional police managers recognized and rewarded those who logged voluntary hours. The predominant criteria for promotions were policing skills and the number of hours worked. There was little value placed on being a competent and effective administrator of human resources.

Our project chief was Ari Oosthoek, a brilliant young inspector with a master's degree in sociology. His forte was statistics and mathematical formulae, and his manner of speaking and writing were almost beyond the comprehension of the common man. He was an excellent boss with an incisive mind and did not hide behind his rank. He insisted on candour from his team, listened carefully to feedback and gave credit where credit was due.

The research team travelled to all parts of Canada, interviewing hundreds of members of the RCMP from all ranks and representing as many facets of the Force as possible. When all the data from our study on overtime compensation were cobbled together, we knew how the report was written would be critical to its acceptance by senior management of the RCMP. Inspector Oosthoek wrote the first draft and gathered his team to discuss it. There was an awkward silence in the room, as we all were of the same mind. The report contained so much academic jargon and so many complex statistics that it smothered the reader. We knew if it went out as Ari had put it together, the senior executive of the Force would never absorb it. We also knew the inspector had spent many hours writing the draft, and we were reluctant to criticize it. Finally, Bill Bovey, one of the civilian members of Planning Branch and a veteran of many similar collaborations, turned to Ari and said, "It won't fly, Sir. It has too much Oosthoekese!"

There was a brief, uncomfortable pause before the inspector's face broke into a grin and he replied, "You're right on the money, Bill. Now let's get to work and put something together that the layperson will be able to read." Thus began long, arduous sessions of putting Inspector

Oosthoek's very valuable and relevant data into a comprehensible package. It illustrated how well a team can work together, and the format we established was applicable to subsequent projects. As it turned out, Inspector Oosthoek's report recommended that overtime compensation be implemented forthwith, and senior management of the Force endorsed his position.

Implementation became another complex issue, and it took two or three years before it was resolved. In the first instance, a lump-sum payment to all was considered; then management flirted with the option of paying these lump sums only to field personnel. Next, the option of paying lieu hours was considered. Finally, a form was designed for hourly compensation. The concept was greeted with great skepticism, and some subdivision OCs forbade the submission of overtime claims. The Division Representative System became active, lobbying and representing members submitting grievances for unpaid overtime. Around 1977 a system of precise payment of overtime hours worked was implemented.

Overtime payments soon began to have an impact on both individual members and the organization. In order to cope with the requirement to pay overtime, the Force concentrated on more efficient shifting of human resources. The organization transformed in ways never imagined by the veterans, as commanders were compelled to work within human resource budgets. The requirement to pay overtime inflicted budgetary chaos upon an organization that had always enjoyed seemingly unlimited free labour.

With no bottomless pit of manpower, unit commanders were compelled to prioritize incoming calls for service. A classic example was the community's expectation of immediate response to private and business alarms. With the proliferation of electronic alarm systems, frequent false alerts became a problem. It was necessary to restrict police attendance to such calls. This led to the appearance of new security firms to fill in for police who no longer had the resources to respond. These developments were only the opening salvo for harried detachment commanders. The first ominous cracks began to appear in the previously unassailable RCMP reputation. After the introduction of overtime, the RCMP would never again achieve adequate human resources to sufficiently compensate for the thousands of gratis hours dedicated personnel worked in the past. It was as if half of the operational complement had just walked out the door and left a very large and unexpected outstanding bill in its wake. Something would have to give, and administrators were not sure how it would all unfold.

As the Force emerged into the world of finite human resources, traditionalists decried the death of *esprit des corps*. Members completed their duties during their shifts and went home instead of hanging around the office waiting for the phone to ring. Yet, interestingly, having the benefit of fresh personnel coming on shift to deal with incoming investigations and complaints enhanced professionalism. Traditionally, life in the Force had been regarded as a vocation akin to the priesthood, but now members began to enjoy life away from the job, with many adopting healthier lifestyles. With more disposable income due to overtime, they were free to marry earlier and accumulate the trappings of married life, including homes and mortgages. The long-held rituals of back-room beer bashes were losing their attraction. Members with young children and wives to support and lawns to cut now had competing priorities.

In addition to the payment of overtime, an important organizational change occurred within the RCMP when women donned the storied red serge and began to serve as regular members in 1975. This momentous decision would have an irreversible impact on the Force in ways never anticipated or expected. From the moment the first female recruit entered the training grounds in Regina, policy makers began to discover factors they had overlooked. Incorporating women in the ranks was largely a process of trial and error, which gave the appearance that the organization had not consulted with other police forces that had included women earlier. The first indoctrination troops to include women were solely female, but later they were trained in troops with men. Dormitories and washroom facilities were inadequate, and the first female uniforms were poorly designed, with flaws eventually identified and changed over a period of years. The entire training division seemed to heave with awkwardness and discomfort. When the first women graduated and were dispersed across the country, supervisors either did not want women on the worksite or tried to be overprotective. Wives of serving members contributed to the negative reception by expressing their discomfort and dissatisfaction with having their spouses working with women. Indeed, the first female RCMP members entered an organization that was not ready for them.

Other important changes had occurred during the early 1970s. At this time, dissatisfaction with working conditions erupted into open rebellion across the Force. Several members were advocating the formation of a union, and the masses were listening. Overtime was not yet being paid, members on call were not reimbursed and too many worksites were understaffed. Commissioner Maurice Nadon appointed several senior officers to travel across the country and listen to the grievances of members. As a result of these meetings, serving members were elected as division representatives by their peers. They were given full-time duties to listen to complaints and advance these to management. Today, staff relations representatives monitor member concerns, sit on committees for pay review and kit and clothing, and generally have freedom to express criticism. The existence of this system has averted the formation of a union or association within the RCMP to this day, and many police forces around the world have studied this model.

My brief period as a researcher acquainted me with the many facets of headquarters in Ottawa and gave me a much broader understanding of how all the pieces might fit into this amazing bureaucratic puzzle. Shortly after my arrival in the capital, I became interested in the Canadian Police College. The college was expanding into a modern, comprehensive campus and was the model for management and communications training for police forces across Canada. Many of my former Depot co-workers taught at the college, and when I was approached to join I transferred from research back into the training business. It was the beginning of the most exciting phase of my training career. Upon entering the CPC as a staff member, my experience as an instructor in Depot qualified me to join the communications staff, teaching potential instructors who were preparing for rotation into Depot. Then, because I had completed several university courses, I was quickly absorbed into the management training unit. Back when I was an instructor in Depot, the elite aces from the management training unit of CPC Ottawa had visited Regina to conduct management courses for municipal police departments. I had been awestruck by their skill and panache, never presuming that one day I would be one of them.

Already intimidated at the prospect of lecturing senior NCOs from police forces across the dominion, I was assigned to teach complex management topics. I had to learn while I earned; minimal time was set aside for indoctrination and preparation, and I had to adapt quickly or suffer the consequences. A novice lecturer like me could easily become isolated if I disputed a point with a single candidate and the other class members took his side. If challenged, I found it useful to solicit input from the group and hope that members of the class would support my position.

I also quickly realized that it was unwise to preach to this experienced cadre of policemen. I had to assure candidates at the outset that I was acting solely as a catalyst in the pursuit of greater knowledge. These experienced police officers did not suffer fools gladly and were liable to lock an instructor out of his own lecture room if they didn't agree with his position or teaching methods. Those of us who were fortunate enough to lead executive development courses involving senior police administrators learned much from the accumulated management experience in the room.

While I was leading a session during a senior police administration course, I shared a strange but poignant moment with one of the candidates. During a break, a candidate named Jack approached me and enquired whether I was the Ian Parsons whose father, Joseph, had also served with the Force. When I said yes, he became emotional, explaining that I had been named after his father, whom he never knew. The story had its roots during the oppressive period in RCMP history when members were forbidden to marry unless they had seven years' service. Many who served during that era were either unable or unwilling to wait and married secretly. After serving for the required time, they anxiously requested approval to marry. Members went to great lengths to conceal their marital status, and often their wives—and sometimes children—resided with parents.

Jack related that his father's first posting had been with my father in Kamsack, Saskatchewan. His father had met the love of his life, and when he moved on to another location they secretly married. Their clandestine life continued pending completion of the seven-year waiting period, but his official marriage application was never to be. While he was assigned mounted duties for a Victoria Day parade, he suffered a massive heart attack, fell off his horse and died in the street. He passed away not realizing his secret wife was pregnant. She remarried, but she insisted that Jack carry the surname of the father he never knew. I was moved by the story and the sequence of events that led to our serendipitous meeting in a CPC classroom.

Soon after, I asked my parents about this other Ian they had known so many years ago. They confirmed the story and were astounded to learn that Ian's son not only carried his father's surname but had also followed his footsteps into the RCMP. My parents had lost track of Ian's wife and had been unaware that he had fathered a child. They told me that young Ian had been an exceptional young policeman with great potential. They were as close as three people could be in a small two-person detachment, often sharing meals, good times and bad. My parents recall being completely devastated by Ian's passing, as he was only 30 years old. Jack returned to his post after completing his studies at the Canadian Police College and served out his time, reaching the rank of staff sergeant, only to die of a heart attack shortly after his retirement. It seemed genetics had visited a similar fate upon the next generation.

Faculty members at CPC were required to travel from time to time to various areas of Canada, where we delivered abbreviated versions of management and instructional topics to police forces on their home turf. While difficult to quantify, it is certain that CPC helped to transform police departments in Canada from autocratic to more participative environments. Thousands of senior police managers were exposed to contemporary management theories and techniques during the 1970s. Time constraints often only allowed us to skim the surface of sophisticated concepts, but the subject material piqued the interest of many and led them to pursue further education. I met candidates at all levels with integrity and devotion to their respective departments, and some became lifelong friends. I found that the professional lecturers selected from all disciplines and walks of life were invaluable in dealing with topics such as human behaviour theory, management dynamics, police–media relations and cross-cultural education. My position as a management resource person at CPC enabled me to pursue these disciplines to an extent almost equivalent to a university degree in human management.

As is so often the case in life, the day-to-day functioning of the college was fraught with irony. Widely known throughout the Canadian police universe, CPC was regarded as the veritable Mecca of contemporary police management theory, yet the college's treatment of its staff did not always reflect participative management. Whereas Inspector George Carter, our immediate superior, was an eloquent, university-educated man and in many ways an inspiring leader, his superior, the assistant director, as well as the college's director, leaned toward the traditional autocratic RCMP leadership style. Inspector Carter was frequently caught between his subordinates and superiors. By the very nature of the curriculum, freedom of thought and innovative approaches had to be encouraged. The dichotomy existed in the rather despotic management environment established by college leaders. Our incoming director had assured his new faculty that the potential for career advancement at the college would be limitless, and he foresaw many of us attaining commissioned rank. But after several years, not one senior NCO instructor had been invited to compete in the officer candidate program.

The faculty at CPC was exclusively RCMP. In order to have the college appear non-partisan, instructors were encouraged to wear civilian clothing while working. In spite of this being an implied requirement, no clothing allowance was granted, even though such allowances were routinely paid to other RCMP members when civilian clothing was deemed an operational necessity. These factors, along with other minor irritations, came to the fore during a staff meeting with our inspector. As the meeting wore on, participants became vocal as their frustrations began to surface. Inspector Carter, obviously feeling the pinch in his position as intermediary, finally retorted, "I might teach this management shit, but I don't have to practise it!" The comment was meant humorously, but he would live with it for the rest of his days as our manager.

The assistant director was a large, bombastic superintendent who was given to bullying. In spite of this, Inspector Carter had the temerity to confront him with our concerns and made some headway. We were fortunate in having Dr. William Kelloway, a renowned and respected psychologist, seconded to the college. In his civilian capacity, he could speak to upper management with candour. His observations about the sometimes toxic management environment at the college had considerable impact on our leaders. They responded to Kelloway's suggestions, changing their approach and improving communication.

CAUGHT WITH THEIR PANTS DOWN

The director of the CPC was an educated, upwardly mobile executive. At the time, there were even rumours of his eventual ascendancy to the commissioner's position. Perhaps aware of this possibility, he seized opportunities to ensure his high profile. Ottawa was hosting a worldwide symposium on policing, and part of the itinerary of the international candidates was a tour of the Canadian Police College. One of the showpieces of the college was the 100-seat auditorium with a large stage, retractable video screen, sloped floor and comfortable tiered seats.

Coincidentally, a group of American and Canadian police had gathered at the college for an organized-crime seminar. During the '70s, the shocking pornographic movie *Deep Throat* was being shown in movie theatres in the USA, and one of the investigators had a copy of the movie. Strictly for "investigative reasons," the candidates wished to view the controversial flick. The course coordinator arranged to gather his flock in the auditorium for an after-hours viewing. Unfortunately, the CPC director was escorting the police leaders through the college at the same time. One can only imagine his shock and that of his guests when he proudly opened the door of the auditorium to be greeted by Linda Lovelace and Harry Reems performing sexual gymnastics on the big screen. The following day, the coordinator of the crime seminar incurred considerable wrath. The CPC director never did reach the dizzy height of commissioner. We often mused with some humour that perhaps this racy choice of after-hours viewing had tipped the scales against him.

While teaching at CPC, I had the good fortune to participate in an instructor exchange program between the college and the FBI Academy in Quantico, Virginia. CPC instructors presented their routine sessions at Quantico for a two-week period, and were replaced by an FBI lecturer at CPC. Personnel at the FBI Academy were extremely receptive and went out of their way to make us feel at home. The contrast in educational qualifications between the two agencies spoke volumes. At a minimum, FBI personnel needed a master's degree, and many of them were working toward their PhDs. In contrast, few RCMP faculty members at CPC had completed a bachelor's degree. Nevertheless, the FBI personnel were impressed by how well RCMP members presented sophisticated material. The content of subject blocks such as management systems, motivation, perception, counselling and interviewing were almost identical at each training centre. The primary difference was the level of formal education of the presenters. When these disparities were reported to RCMP management, efforts were made to upgrade the faculty's educational levels to achieve parity with institutes such as the FBI Academy, but even today very few CPC instructors possess advanced degrees.

While I was serving at CPC, the position of chief academic instructor at the RCMP Academy in Regina became available. The job offered a promotion to staff sergeant. I was approaching 20 years' service in the Force and hoped to be located in the western half of the country when the time came to retire, so I applied for the highly sought-after position, as did many of my peers. My comprehensive background in RCMP training at all levels, together with my field service and recently acquired bachelor's degree, contributed to my attaining the post.

CHAPTER II

DÉJÀ VU

In the spring of 1980, I returned to Regina to take up my new position. The Academy had continued its transition to more sophisticated methodology since my tour of duty as an instructor in the 1970s. The recruit experience of the 1980s was light years ahead of my own experience in 1961. Externally, the trappings and appearances of Depot remained the same. Recruits still moved about in troop formation, marching smartly. Foot drill was still a part of the curriculum, and noon parades were priorities. The fundamental differences were in the classroom and the gym, where the emphasis was on simulation and scenario training and physical conditioning.

In my new position, I supervised over 30 junior NCO instructors working out of five distinct academic units. The instructors' immediate supervisors were sergeants, who reported to me. It was the most complex management structure I had encountered thus far. The academic section had its own modern building designed for contemporary studies. It was a dynamic, exhilarating environment. The instructors were highly motivated and self-directed, which made my job an easy one. The *esprit de corps* and morale within the section were high, with the possibility of hijinks never far from the surface.

BILINGUALISM?

The sergeant major in an RCMP training division occupies a high-profile position. He literally "sets the tone," metes out discipline, supervises the instructors and is generally involved in all decisions pertaining to training. One such sergeant major who presided at Depot was a man who typically turned himself out impeccably. Accompanying this attention to detail were somewhat unique expressions of pronunciation and vocabulary. We never knew whether these peculiarities were intended humorously or done unintentionally.

When referring to the aggregate of classical musicians in downtown Regina, the sergeant major referred to them as the Regina Sympathy Orchestra. The bass drummer of the Depot bugle band wore the skin of an exotic cat as an apron over his uniform, as is the custom in military bands. When not in use, it hung in the sergeant major's office. He proudly described it as the leotard skin.

Another example of his occasional lack of verbal acuity occurred when one of the troop supervisors prepared a letter of resignation on behalf of a departing recruit. The recruit in question was homesick and was determined to be full of nostalgia. Upon reading the memo, the sergeant major enquired about the young man's condition of "nostaleegia," wanting to be sure that he received the proper medical attention for his affliction.

During this senior NCO's tenure, there had been a series of rumours circulating in the training division. After a daily noon parade, the instructors formed up in troop formation, as the sergeant major wished to address all personnel. Everyone stood at attention. He paced up and down the ranks, and in a stentorian voice lectured on the evils of spreading untruths. As he reached the climax of his message, he roared, "There's been a whole lot of allegations going around here, and if I ever catch the ALLIGATORS . . ." There was silence from the troop, followed by snickers, then peals of laughter. The division disciplinarian had lost his audience in the blink of an eye.

This man was also renowned for his discomfort around technology. The training division had recently acquired a paper shredder, which was located next to the photocopy machine. The commanding officer had just prepared a memo and was about to make a duplicate. The sergeant major, anxious to illustrate his newfound skills and accommodate his superior, took the freshly typed original memo from the hands of the CO and promptly put it through the shredder.

Although his mangling of the Queen's English and penchant for gaffes were well known, this man was fondly respected for his humanity, lack of airs and good spirits. He continued in his position of sergeant major for several years, and retired after a full career of training RCMP recruits.

My own tour of Depot as an instructor had concluded just prior to the introduction of female recruits. When I returned in 1980, the changes were obvious, even though the co-ed academy was still a recent development and the first female instructor was yet to arrive. Perhaps this was the reason for the occasional regression of attitude on the part of the male instructors.

Reg Potsby, the sergeant in charge of the law unit, viewed himself as a "liberated man," but his occasionally lascivious comments during lectures clearly displayed a chauvinistic bent. One of the older and worldlier female recruits had a curious artistic ability; she could fashion the most life-like human penises from nylon stockings. While not a skill in great demand, it was a source of hilarity among the female troops. The corporals assigned to the law unit learned of this talent and asked her to fashion a gigantic one. Unbeknownst to Sergeant Potsby, an elaborate suspension system was fashioned along the upper portion of the chalkboard at the front of his classroom. While the sergeant was waxing eloquent in front of a female class, the large penis, controlled from outside the classroom, was pulled across the room on the string, coming to rest above him. Potsby's audience fell into hysterical laughter, gesturing toward the object sitting just above the sergeant's head. Even though he appeared to enjoy the stunt, Potsby lost control of the class and had to dismiss his students early. His mischievous corporals had second thoughts in weeks to come when they encountered drawers glued shut, false memos indicating their transfers to Inuvik and phone calls from a local escort service. As is so often the case in such situations, the boss always wins; however, in retrospect, I can see that the incident prompted the sergeant to reconsider his demeanour with female students.

EACH SPRING SAW a new crop of instructors arrive from the field as senior members rotated back to operational duties. The arrival of a constable from Montreal exemplified how unprepared the RCMP were in dealing with members surfacing from undercover duties. Brad Dalton had been performing undercover work in Montreal for about two years, participating in a large and complex drug operation. There is perhaps no other duty in police work that takes such a psychological toll. While undercover, agents must eat, live and breathe in the most primitive conditions. Their lives are constantly in danger, particularly if their true identities are discovered. When undercover members surface, they are dirty, dishevelled, disoriented and traumatized. After Dalton's undercover assignment ended, it was felt that his life was in danger, so instead of having the opportunity to debrief and rehabilitate, he was immediately transferred to the training division.

Dalton was expected to present himself as a squeaky-clean role model for recruits, but his classroom demeanour soon revealed how unsuited he was for a training environment. His mannerisms disturbed his recruit students. While he quickly assumed all the physical requirements of an ideal instructor, dressing smartly, replete with gleaming leather and impeccable grooming, his language was coarse, sometimes peppered with obscene street jargon. Senior management members were shocked by Dalton's behaviour and moved to intervene. When they made preparations to remove him from his teaching role, I spoke on his behalf, reminding them of the young man's background and outlining the trauma of protracted undercover operations. Although his promotion to corporal was deferred, Dalton was permitted to remain on staff. He was closely supervised and tutored over a period of time. He eventually curbed his raunchy tongue and slowly began to behave in a more acceptable manner.

I realized some years later that I had overlooked symptoms of post-traumatic stress manifested by another instructor, Grant Lortie. But I wasn't the only one. Trained psychologists working in the academic section, along with many of the man's peers who had training in human behaviour, also failed to identify what Lortie was experiencing. Lortie had been stationed on a municipal detail in Nanaimo, British Columbia. One evening while he was assigned to the detachment complaint desk, a co-worker had arrested an individual for impaired driving. When released, the citizen went home and returned to the detachment with a 12-gauge shotgun concealed under his overcoat. He entered the office and stood at the complaint counter. When Constable Lortie approached him, the man pulled the shotgun from his coat and fired, striking Lortie in the abdomen. Seriously injured, Lortie managed to talk the assailant into dropping his gun. After a brief exchange, the shooter seemed to regret his actions and even drove Lortie to the hospital for treatment. He was quickly taken into custody and arrested for attempted murder.

Lortie arrived at the Academy some years later, having physically recovered from his wound. He was the epitome of a policeman—six foot three inches tall, well built and very impressive in uniform. He was also a capable instructor and considered to be one of the comers in the section. Although he projected well in the classroom and was highly respected by his troops, Lortie was closed and uncommunicative with peers and supervisors. I monitored each instructor annually, attending one of their presentations and then debriefing them. It gave me an opportunity to question them on their careers and aspirations. During my interviews with Lortie, he was tense, answering questions in a terse manner and offering little from his personal perspective. It was obvious that he wanted to terminate the interview as soon as possible.

When I talked about his potential and the possibility of his pursuing extra education, Lortie's responses were muted, making it difficult to establish any rapport with him. He continued to perform his job in an exemplary fashion and rotated out after his three years at the Academy.

Corporal Lortie returned to operational duties in British Columbia, and the occasional news I would receive about him was not favourable. Several years later, I learned that Lortie's marriage had failed. He had also been subject to a service investigation after refusing to wear his sidearm on duty and been found derelict in responding to a public complaint. The details related to me seemed highly out of character. Lortie subsequently retired, never rising above the rank of corporal. It was a most disappointing end to a career that had once appeared so promising. Following his retirement, Lortie settled in a remote community and became reclusive. I later learned that one of his daughters, a registered psychiatric nurse, always suspected her Dad was concealing unresolved issues. She finally persuaded her father to release his demons, and he disclosed that he was haunted by the shooting incident. No therapy or counselling had been offered to him after the event, as the Force was just becoming aware of post-traumatic stress disorder (PTSD) and little assistance was in place for shooting incident survivors. Corporal Lortie finally received some psychiatric help and a disability pension. In retrospect, it was obvious he was a casualty of a stressful occupation that failed to provide the necessary compassionate attention. This unfortunate history emphasizes the absolute necessity for supervisors in high-risk occupations such as law enforcement to be proactive when it comes to dealing with the trauma their employees are experiencing. In recent years, the Force has implemented many positive changes in the debriefing of members returning to uniform duty from undercover work and in the diagnosis and treatment of PTSD.

IN TODAY'S RCMP ACADEMY, computers are ubiquitous and instructors engage in animated classroom exchanges with students, who are encouraged to debate and doubt. Spearheaded by a cadre of talented, educated junior NCOs, the human-relations program has grown from the modest 18 hours first proposed in the early 1970s to over 200 hours, with successful candidates receiving university credits from the University of Regina. It is gratifying to know that I was involved in introducing this vital facet of police training, and it was icing on the cake to return to the Academy a second time and expand the program further.

Cynical veterans still denigrate the human-relations program and training in general, as they have done since the inception of the Force in 1873. Each successive generation seems to believe that current basic training is never as tough or as good as that experienced by the previous old guard. Even after the physically cruel experience of my own era, we encountered veterans who assured us that their horses were tougher and their instructors meaner than anything we had to contend with.

Current RCMP training puts greater emphasis on academia, but the physical-training and driver-training sections are equally important. The primary objective in contemporary police training is the dovetailing of all disciplines, and much of the basic recruit-training curriculum now appears under the umbrella of "Applied Police Sciences." There is no tolerance for individual sections teaching solely to their course training standards and ignoring everything else in the curriculum. One thing has not changed, however: there are never enough hours in the day for recruits. Interestingly, expectations of performance are higher than ever. The setting and achieving of personal goals are paramount in today's RCMP Academy.

Although it has been many years since my tenure at the RCMP Academy, there is still a family connection to this day. My daughter, Michelle, who has degrees in social work, is an assistant supervisor working within the Saskatchewan Ministry of Justice, Young Offender Programs, Corrections and Policing. Michelle lectures to RCMP recruits about her role in the justice system dealing with law enforcement relating to young offenders.

As my tour at the Academy came to an end, I was seriously looking toward retirement from the Force and considering a different line of work. While I was considering my future, my supervising officer approached me about competing for a Queen's Commission, the door that leads to senior management of the Force. The officer corps has always been steeped in tradition and mystique. For years, admission into this exclusive upper echelon was likened to being knighted. We were all conditioned to dream of the remote possibility of reaching this level. As members travelled the lengthy and arduous career highway, many abandoned hope of reaching this pinnacle. There were many reasons for this: lack of preparation, location, marital and family status and cynicism accrued through years of dealing with the flaws of humanity. Because of my father's career, I'd had the opportunity to view the officer corps from the inside, and it held considerable appeal for me.

Historically, candidacy for senior NCOs into the officer corps was initiated by a recommendation from an officer. As the Force entered the 21st century, leaders began to realize that this procedure might not always identify the most appropriate candidates. Although, even today, qualifying for a commission still requires a recommendation by an officer, such a recommendation now follows a rigorous series of hurdles consisting of a four-hour written exam, a research paper and an appearance before a board of senior officers. The candidates, all seasoned RCMP veterans, complete the exam in various locations across the country. Members have been known to peruse this exam and walk out of the room in defeat, and some do not withstand the verbal inquisition of the officer candidate board. When I was a candidate, the aggressive demeanour of some of the officers resembled the approach of instructors of Depot past. To many of us, it was akin to once again running the gauntlet.

A complex points system is used to calculate a candidate's total scores, with annual performance appraisals taken into account. Once the scores are computed, successful candidates are placed on a list and await the telephone call from a representative from Officer's Staffing Branch in Ottawa. A candidate is first asked whether he or she is still mobile and willing to serve anywhere in Canada. If the response is affirmative, he or she receives a posting.

The Officer Candidate Program was extremely stressful for me. I considered with trepidation how I would be able to lead the dynamic young men under my command if I was not successful in my quest for a commission. In the years to follow, 10 out of these 33 members would compete in the Officer Candidate Program. Two became commanding officers, and one attained the level of deputy commissioner. The success rate of this single group from the academic section far surpassed the Force-wide average of 5 percent.

I was fortunate to place second out of 397 successful officer candidates. Once on the list, I waited, hoping for officer vacancies. For 12 months my standing vacillated between number 1 and number 3 as each new batch of officer candidates was added into the list. To complicate matters, this was the era when biculturalism and bilingualism became a priority of the federal government. Departments were urged to redress the imbalance of anglophone versus francophone leaders. The RCMP was no exception, and the commissioner of the day decided to bypass unilingual English officer candidates at the top of the list in favour of those who were bilingual. Incensed, I applied for the position of chief of police in Prince Albert, Saskatchewan. After the initial competition, the department's deputy chief and I remained as the final choices. The deputy won the position, and I continued to await my fate within the RCMP.

CHAPTER 12

AN OFFICER AND A GENTLEMAN?

After almost a year on the officer candidate list, I received my call from Ottawa. I had always wanted to serve in British Columbia, but my caller informed me I would receive a Maritime posting, in Newfoundland. Although devastated by this news, I conceded that it would be folly to refuse when I had gone so far in the process. I accepted and prepared to travel to Newfoundland as a newly minted audit officer. I was to be based in St. John's, and my duties would consist of inspecting detachments and units throughout the province, acting under the direction and on behalf of the commanding officer.

This was also a time of great upheaval in my personal life. Lorraine and I had decided that we would go our separate ways and seek a divorce. Both of our children elected to remain in Regina, so I would be moving to Newfoundland alone.

An avid motorcycle enthusiast for some years, I was a member of the Blue Knights Law Enforcement Motorcycle Club and planned to travel to my new posting via motorcycle. The Blue Knights consist of some 8,000 law-enforcement riders with chapters across North America and Europe. I loaded my large-displacement Yamaha motorcycle with camping gear and struck out for Newfoundland, a distance of 3,000 miles. One of the attractions of travelling by motorcycle is the kinship bikers enjoy. Once dressed in leathers astride a bike, one assumes a measure of anonymity. People from all walks of life take to the road to savour the freedom of the motorcycle lifestyle. As I travelled across Canada, I encountered many of these riders. One evening while I was camped in an RV park, several riders rolled in, apparently members of an outlaw biker gang. Once they had set up camp, one of them strolled over and invited me to share a joint. I declined, pleading an early start in the morning. Life would have become rather interesting had they learned they had offered marijuana to a police officer.

As I travelled across various provinces and states I also experienced the discrimination often encountered by motorcyclists. On more than one occasion, I was turned away from an upscale RV park or motel. Perhaps my unshaven state and large bike contributed to the lack of hospitality. After one exhausting travel day, I needed to show my RCMP identification badge before the motel owner hesitatingly allowed me to lodge in his premises. When I finally arrived at my new Division Headquarters, I was greeted by raised eyebrows and looks of consternation. Even my commanding officer seemed somewhat distressed when he was told his new audit officer had recently arrived via motorcycle.

For the next three years, I lived out of my suitcase, travelling to every nook and cranny of Newfoundland and Labrador. Although there was some culture shock on my part, the people I encountered in my new posting were the kindest, most generous, fun-loving souls on the planet. Living in and travelling across this unique part of Canada gave me a great appreciation of the breadth and diversity of our country.

Shortly after my arrival in St. John's, I had the great good fortune to meet Joan Dooley, a beautiful and vivacious divorced mother of two teenagers. Although she lived in the city, her home and heart rested in the tiny village of Adam's Cove, about 80 miles by road around Conception Bay from St. John's. You could gaze directly across the bay at the lights of St. John's, which was only about 20 miles across the water.

HUMBLE PIE

I am sharing this incident, which was experienced by a friend of mine, as a warning to all who might lose their perspective as they climb the ladder of success. He never forgot the humbling incident, particularly when occasional visions of grandeur slithered into his consciousness.

Some years ago, my friend had the good fortune to receive his commission. In addition to all the other accoutrements of office, he acquired the very distinctive mess kit that only commissioned officers have the privilege to wear. He was preparing to attend a function in Ottawa, his very first event as an officer.

He reverently laid out his new finery, donning the tight-fitting dress overalls known as banana pants, box spurs and congress boots. Then came the pleated white shirt with gold studs, along with a black bow tie. A natty blue waistcoat with tiny miniature regimental buttons was the next item, capped by the splendid scarlet short jacket, topped with two glorious crowns denoting his new rank of inspector. White gloves and the distinguished RCMP officer's forage hat, complete with the shiny black visor and broad gold band denoting the status of a commissioned officer, completed the accoutrements. After ensuring he had forgotten nothing, he departed his residence, glancing in a full-length mirror for a final look. Delighted with the overall appearance, he couldn't help but think to himself that he had finally arrived.

The soiree was being held at the Château Laurier in downtown Ottawa. Unbeknownst to the fledgling officer, Guy Lombardo and his Royal Canadians, a popular dance orchestra, was playing in and around Ottawa. As the new inspector emerged from his vehicle in front of the luxury hotel, a valet appeared to assist in parking. The valet looked the inspector up and down and asked the innocent question that would change everything forever: "You guys playing here tonight?"

On the weekends we travelled to Adam's Cove, where I was able to learn about and appreciate the wonderful Newfoundland people and traditions to a much greater extent than most visiting mainlanders. Joan's father had long passed, but her mother, Marie Hollett, who was as charming as her daughter, always welcomed us fondly.

Our arrival necessitated a community gathering in Marie's large kitchen. As many as a dozen folks would be seated there, sipping Screech and occasionally breaking into song. To my untrained ear, the accents, rapidity of delivery and liberal use of colloquialisms made the conversation unintelligible. Unexpectedly, a machine-gun comment or question would be delivered my way, to which I'd respond, "Yes, of course," never really knowing what I had agreed to. As time went on, my ear developed some appreciation for the dialect, but it was ever a challenge. Seated at the dinner table one night, I passed the bread and my neighbour said, "No thank, moi son, Oim blocked." I initially thought he had a serious intestinal problem, when all he was saying was he was full. When someone else suffered a traffic accident, he told me his car was "all bent op." Then there was the excitement of going out to the "toim" for a "scuff and a scoff." I learned that a "toim" was a good time where one had a dance and a meal.

One afternoon, I was seated in Joan's living room in St. John's when her 14-year-old daughter walked in with a friend. She looked at me and said, "Say sompin, Ian." I looked at her, somewhat puzzled, and asked her what she wanted me to say. She replied, "Anyting, ya talks fonny." The girls giggled and left the room. I sat musing about how it felt to be in such a minority. Another afternoon, Joan wanted to wander in one of the local malls. I had other plans and exhibited some irritation. She looked at me, and in her best Bayman's accent said, "Don't go getting crooked wit me now, or I'll be smackin' the face right off ya!" How could anyone respond negatively to such an attack? I obediently went to the mall with her.

Learning to be a member of the officer corps was another lesson in a new culture. RCMP commissioned officers are clearly a cloister within a cloister. There were unspoken expectations within this exclusive band, and I found that I needed to pay attention to the slightest behavioural nuances. You were expected to have your morning coffee breaks with your brother officers, and it was noted who sat closest to the commanding officer. On Fridays there was usually a social gathering. There were two messes: one for NCOs and constables, the other for officers. Occasionally the two groups would assemble briefly in the NCOs' mess, but almost never in the officers'. The line between officers and everyone else was always present, however subtle. It was a line I had great difficulty maintaining with my audit team. I was the sole officer and was initially treated with deference. However, as time went on we became very close and much of this stilted atmosphere dissipated. The game was certainly played while we conducted our business, but it seldom showed when we were not in session. I was absent from Division Headquarters much of the time with my audit team, so this delayed my indoctrination as an officer. The aura surrounding commissioned officers is another prevailing remnant of the "Olden Force," even though the demands of a modern police organization have eliminated some of the former aloofness and separation.

Chief Superintendent J.B. "Dale" Henry, the commanding officer, was an insular man, steeped in the old tradition and placing little value in trivia or frivolity. He was egocentric and expected the policing universe to revolve around him. To Henry's credit, he was very bright and capable—perhaps the most competent officer I served under during my commissioned years. My tenure with him spanned six years; we served in the Maritimes together, then proceeded to Manitoba for three more years. Consequently, two-thirds of my officer career was influenced by him. Chief Superintendent Henry was a consummate politician, who exhibited poise and ease when dealing with all levels of government. He knew his job thoroughly and in many ways exemplified an RCMP division commander. His preparation and attention to detail became obvious as we flew together to Newfoundland detachments to debrief his commanders after an audit. While I read my motorcycle magazine, Henry pored over files relating to the worksite we were about to visit. Upon our arrival, I learned the reason for his preparation. He would stop and greet constables by their first names, asking them how a specific investigation was going. These young men and women were astounded that their commanding officer had such intimate knowledge of their names and their work.

Henry tended to be a user, harvesting every iota of talent from subordinates and giving little in return. He expected dedication and consummate performance but rarely recognized exceptional service. His demeanour seemed to convey that any effort you expended was never quite sufficient. One could learn much from his ability as an organizer, but less in the way of stroking, nurturing and encouraging. To his credit, Henry was not a micromanager. If you had his confidence, you were granted ample latitude to perform tasks. Conversely, if he discovered his faith in you was misdirected, you would find yourself relegated to a position of minimal responsibility, or even subject to a transfer.

WHILE IN THE Training Division in Regina, I had assisted in forming a Blue Knights chapter. Having enjoyed being part of the group in the past, at my new posting I joined the St. John's chapter. It consisted largely of members of the local municipal police force, which gave me an opportunity to get to know them. These connections would work to my advantage in my capacity as audit officer. As a group, we travelled to Bangor, Maine, to attend an international Blue Knights rally in the summer of 1986. Almost 3,000 riders from the law-enforcement community gathered for the event, coming from all parts of the USA and Canada. It was amazing to witness the Knights ride through the city of Bangor in formation, a sea of powder-blue vests with the distinctive Blue Knights logo.

The founders of the Blue Knights crafted a crest featuring a blue knight carrying a lance and sitting astride a motorcycle. A top and bottom rocker surrounded the crest. The top rocker identifies the Blue Knights, while the bottom designates the home chapter. This configuration is similar to outlaw biker crests and was meant to counteract the negative image by replacing the undesirable with something desirable. But the similarity in crest design is where any likeness to the outlaws ends. Blue Knight members wear powder-blue, police-style motorcycle helmets. They practise and promote safe motorcycle operation and project an image of goodwill and cooperation to the driving public. Even so, the arrival of a Blue Knights chapter on their big bikes may be intimidating until spectators learn that the riders are law-enforcement officers.

Occasionally, an undesirable minority skews this positive message. An American Blue Knights chapter appeared at the rally in Bangor with a design on their jackets that was offensive and troubling to all. The crest worn on their vests depicted an unauthorized death's head or skull in place of the Blue Knight logo. They rode loud, unmuffled Harley Davidson bikes, obviously emulating the outlaws. The Blue Knights International Executive directed them to remove the offensive crests immediately, but they refused. They were summarily banned from all rally events and stripped of their chapter. It was clear the Blue Knights wanted any implied connection to the outlaw biker world eradicated.

MY WORK IN Newfoundland immersed me in the fractious world of internal audit. As audit officer, I was charged with examining all activities occurring within the RCMP operation in the province, essentially "taking the pulse" of the organization on behalf of the commanding officer. He headed the audit committee, which was composed of his divisional officers. This committee would decree who, where and what the audit team would examine. We were also responsible for assessing the level of public satisfaction. Our work took us to all corners of the province, and we were on the road much of the year. Once the data were collected, a report was submitted to the audit committee with findings and recommendations.

Unavoidably, the audit was negative, since the team was searching for noncompliance. Accordingly, the targets were not generally delighted when we appeared, and many received our assurance that "We're here to help you" with cynicism and raised eyebrows. I soon learned that a good audit officer had to dedicate some of his time to alleviating his clients' anxieties. The audit officer's personality set the tone and had everything to do with the acceptance of the audit. I found that having a sense of humour and keeping things light during the process went a long way toward reducing stress.

A certain amount of tact was needed when determining which findings could be resolved locally and which should go into the audit report. The commanding officer suggested that several experienced field supervisors should be placed on a list and rotated through the audit team. We found that these individuals' presence brought familiarity and increased our credibility. In addition, the participating field supervisors developed empathy for the auditors.

No matter how hard we tried to alleviate the stress of our appearance on the doorstep of a detachment, the audit experience was an ordeal for both for the auditee and the auditors. The conclusion of the exercise was a relief to all, and occasionally team members would blow off a bit of steam when it was all over. No doubt detachment members also did so after our departure. In September 1984, we had travelled by commercial aircraft from Corner Brook to Gander during Pope John Paul II's Canadian visit. Newfoundland was his next destination. The papal visit was saturating the news media across the land, and there were numerous television segments showing the pope exiting an aircraft and prostrating himself on the tarmac to kiss the ground. As we left the aircraft in Gander, one of the audit team members, Spud Gallant, emulated the pope, falling to his knees and kissing the ground, then turning around to his amazed fellow passengers and uttering, "Thank you for the gifts," a phrase also used by the pope. We were thankful that day that no one on the plane knew who we were.

On another occasion we visited the isolated community of Harbour Breton on the extreme south coast. After a long drive, we arrived at noon and started looking for a place to have lunch. The corporal directed us to the only establishment in town that catered to visitors. When we arrived, we found the place locked and a sign reading, "Out to Lunch." Only in Newfoundland! That day we dined on potato chips and Pepsi. We also visited Burgeo, a town on the south coast made famous by author Farley Mowat. Just off the coast was Ramea Island, housing the small community of Ramea. I mentioned to Corporal McGuire, the NCO in charge, that I would like to visit Ramea. He informed me that it was a "mite lumpy" out there today. I glanced at the harbour and assured him I was comfortable in rough water. He raised his eyebrows but agreed to ferry me to Ramea in the detachment boat, a solid-looking Boston Whaler with twin outboards. As we made our way out of the harbour I was puzzled that Corporal McGuire had been hesitant, as the water was quite calm. About a mile out to sea, we began to encounter increasingly large waves of 12 feet or more. As the boat was tossed around vigorously, I told McGuire that I now understood what he meant by "a mite lumpy." However, we now seemed committed to our course, and it appeared that it would be difficult to turn around in the rough seas. The corporal waited for exactly the right moment, then cramped the steering hard and leaned on the throttle. The boat wheeled around in the trough, and we headed back to the harbour. I had learned first-hand the power and danger of the North Atlantic.

The resourcefulness of RCMP members at isolated postings has always amazed me. We had included Hopedale Detachment as part of our audit sample. Situated on the east coast of Labrador, Hopedale could be the most isolated detachment in all of Canada. The detachment building is far and away the most modern structure in the community, which has a predominately Native population and also includes a Moravian mission. A corporal, his wife and two single members are stationed there. We arrived in the RCMP helicopter, and as I entered the detachment I noted a wheelbarrow parked by the door. It was painted in regimental blue and gold and had a crest on it. The corporal informed me the wheelbarrow was the detachment paddy wagon. There are no roads in the community, so if there was a report of an intoxicated person, the wheelbarrow was activated to retrieve the prisoner. There were no provisions for this conveyance in policy, but it was not made a subject of the audit report.

Each year, the division commander summoned his officers located throughout Newfoundland and Labrador to assemble in St. John's to attend a Program Oriented Work Planning Meeting. In bureaucratese, this activity is referred to as a POWPM, not to be confused with powwow, even though there are similarities. At the gathering, the CO communicated his priorities and wishes and pontificated on the state of policing in the province. The RCMP's internal managerial review process had recently been altered, and the CO requested that I make a presentation, as reviews fell under the purview of audit. Even though I had much experience speaking in front of groups, I was understandably edgy when it came to addressing my brother officers. The session was going well until one of my audience asked how frequently the managerial reviews were to be completed. Instead of using the word "yearly," I chose to respond by stating "annually." For reasons I will never fully understand, the word came out as "anally." There was a brief silence, then pandemonium. I was barraged with trite observations such as, "Does that mean the audit officer is anally retentive?" Even the CO put in his two cents' worth. I had lost my audience, and I was thankful my gaffe came at the conclusion of my presentation. I believe that was the moment I acquired a measure of infamy.

My duties as audit officer also led to confrontations not unlike those experienced by Henry Kissinger, the great conciliator and former US secretary of state. One such case involved a feisty subdivision commander and the Charter of Rights and Freedoms, which came into force as part of the Constitution Act of 1982 and changed many everyday policing procedures. As it was new legislation, the commissioner had recently urged all of his COs across the nation to ensure compliance with the Charter. Accordingly, Chief Superintendent Henry had made it an audit priority. During the audit, we realized that a particular subdivision was not paying due diligence to certain aspects of the legislation. I discussed this informally with Inspector Clyde Courser, the inspector in charge of the subdivision. His amazing response to me was that he did not believe in or subscribe to the Charter, and it would never come into being in the province of Newfoundland. His next comment was, "You people from away should stop telling us how to do our job!" ("Come from away" is a Newfoundland colloquialism describing anyone not born and bred in the province.) Astounded, I said that if he were not prepared to retract his comments and begin complying with the legislation, I would be forced to make a formal finding in the audit report and further advise the commanding officer. Courser's response was "Fill your boots!"

When I got back to headquarters, I briefed the commanding officer. Shocked, he suggested I might have misunderstood. He summoned Inspector Courser to appear before him forthwith. The inspector appeared and repeated his audacious comments to the commanding officer. The two combatants had known each other for most of their service and had long held diverging philosophies. There was little love lost between them, and during this encounter in the CO's office, I felt like I was watching an enraged ball player in dispute with an umpire. The inspector's comments had clearly become insubordinate, and he departed briskly. Chief Superintendent Henry contacted the commissioner in Ottawa to tell him what had occurred. Inspector Courser was personally contacted by the commissioner and commanded to comply with the requirements of the Charter of Rights and Freedoms immediately. He complied but subsequently resigned his commission and left the Force. It was a classic example of the suicidal defiance for which this officer was known. His rebelliousness had finally done him in. Interestingly, he attended university after leaving the Force and eventually obtained a law degree. It occurred to me that he had already decided his future prior to the audit and had decided to leave in a blaze of glory. Although confrontations during an audit were not common, they occurred frequently enough to make the job interesting.

Clyde Courser was clearly an anomaly within the officer corps. I have noticed a most curious transformation that occurs when one is honoured with the Queen's Commission within a police organization. Members who have confronted daunting situations during their ascent up the law-enforcement ladder seem to misplace their intestinal fortitude upon becoming officers. These are individuals who have faced down rowdy barrooms full of drunks, been outnumbered and unbowed by outlaw biker gangs and placed in many circumstances where their personal courage has been tested. This courage is not only physical, as many of them have been harangued by intimidating lawyers, overbearing politicians and anti-social members of the public.

Yet the assertiveness and presence of mind that served these public servants so well seems to diminish with the assumption of executive rank. Is this because senior officers have learned the power of intimidation as they experienced it on their own personal ascent? I learned that the officer's handbook outlined the courtesy of writing a letter to the commissioner to thank him for conferring the honour of a commission upon one's humble person. This was still expected in spite of the gauntlet of screening, writing an exam, appearing before two levels of oral boards and preparing a lengthy paper. A path of rigorous personal preparation had replaced the old procedure of being solely endorsed by an officer; however, the requirement to thank the commissioner was still a necessity. It didn't surprise me that many of the newly commissioned neglected to comply.

Analyzing the group dynamics of a typical police executive committee is as good a way as any to observe the hierarchy at work. These assemblies are usually highly confidential and can be found in session in command centres across the country. They consist of the commanding officer or chief constable, who is typically the chairman.

Seated at the table are senior and junior officers who command some segment of the police operation. The commanding officer sets the agenda. Members of the committee will bring items to the table from time to time, but it is primarily a forum from which the commanding officer expresses his insights and philosophies on how his operation will be run. Opinions are welcome—providing they support or endorse the CO's position. Dissenting views are considered somewhat of an inconvenience and can shine an uncomfortable light upon the originator. Former independent thinkers spend much time anticipating what the CO wants to hear, because that is what is acceptable.

There are many unspoken messages that must be gleaned and understood within the officer corps, and it can be a rather steep learning curve for the neophyte. I knew of one case where the CO would often return to his office after the supper hour to continue his weighty work. All of his underlings were aware of this habit, and several made a point of staying at their work stations until "Himself" departed for the evening. One member of the team often sat at his desk reading a paperback. He had no reason to be in his office other than the fact that the CO was on site. Many felt they had to be available in the event the great man needed to confer.

Another CO was very social and expected his minions to be on hand at the officer's mess for any and all occasions. Dignitaries and even entertainers who had little or no relevance to the police operation were invited to dine, and the CO advised his officers that they were expected to be there, often in uniform. The mess would have a full complement for the evening, no questions asked. This occurred several times a month, but very few had the effrontery to decline these command performances.

This servility within the officer corps has diminished, but it still exists. Most commissioned officers will not challenge the CO, even if they disagree with his policy. This reluctance to speak up does not make for a dynamic organization and may be the reason police forces are so slow to change. Most successful COs have been through the RCMP acculturation process, and many expect the same fealty that was required of them during their ascension.

Although we no longer conclude our correspondence with the phrase, "I have the honour to be, Sir, your obedient servant," the tradition of conferring supreme power on the CO is alive and well. Having been a member of the "League of Frightened Men," I have personally experienced these dynamics to a greater or lesser degree. They can pervade any corporate structure, but the paramilitary model of law enforcement predisposes this type of intimidation. It is entirely possible that this model, which served the RCMP so well in 1873, no longer meets organizational needs. In fact, in the 21st century a military hierarchy may be the worst possible model for the Force. Toward the end of my career, in about 1990, the officers were issued sparkling white shirts to distinguish them further from the ranks, who wore khaki-coloured shirts. I recall being referred to as a "white shirt" in what I perceived to be a spirit of good nature. Now when I hear members refer to "white shirts," it usually has a negative connotation.

There are many examples of how the commissioned officer cadre indelibly stamps its members, some of whom should have had their rank insignia tattooed on their skin. In Victoria, BC, a veritable boneyard of retired officers continue to enjoy their station through retirement and beyond. There is a retired officer's mess where the gentlemen can assemble and commiserate with one another without having to worry about "the lads." This is indicative of the mindset of many commissioned members and illustrates how persistent these barriers to forthright communication can be. In today's complex world, trying to run an efficient, effective organization with the restrictions of a military rank structure is surely a recipe for failure. It is incumbent on any chief executive of a police force in the 21st century to banish this suffocating environment in the interest of generating fresh ideas and innovative thought.

CHAPTER 13

HALFWAY HOME

Upon returning to St. John's from one of my many work excursions, I learned that Joan Dooley had been diagnosed with breast cancer. It was the beginning of a terrible trial for her. She immediately received the necessary surgery, followed by the ordeal of radiation and chemotherapy. Over several harrowing months, she demonstrated unequalled courage and optimism. I remained at her side through it all, and when it appeared that she was in remission, I made the decision to transfer to Manitoba. My father was in failing health in Victoria, and I wanted to be closer in the event he took a turn for the worse. Shortly after my transfer, I learned that Joan was again ill. I returned to St. John's to be with her. I remained as long as I could but eventually had to return to my duties. Not long after I left St. John's, Joan lost her battle. Being part of her struggle and witnessing her courage through it all affected me as no other experience had ever done. After sharing her agonizing journey, I emerged a deeper and more thoughtful human being.

My next position was destined to be a welcome challenge in the field of operations. A new subdivision was being established in southwestern Manitoba, headquartered in the small rural community of Carman. I looked forward to returning to prairie policing. I arrived in the summer of 1986, finding nothing but an empty room in the post office building that would be my headquarters. I would be building the infrastructure from scratch and needed to acquire furniture, initiate filing systems and, most importantly, find a clerk/stenographer.

The reorganization addressed the large and unwieldy structure that existed in the province at the time. Winnipeg subdivision, one of the largest in Canada, was being divided into four small, independent subdivisions that would consist of several detachments totalling about 100 personnel. It was an advantage to have arrived in the province with my former commanding officer in Newfoundland, Dale Henry. Our shared work history had given him confidence in me, and I was left largely to my own devices.

Problems quickly became evident at two of the larger detachments. The former subdivision had become so massive that detachments were not being monitored adequately. One of the detachment commanders had developed mental health problems, creating a mutinous environment. It was another sad example of detachment personnel being intimidated by seniority and rank and continuing to function under the most bizarre of work settings. After probing the operation, I learned of strange incidents of paranoia on the part of the NCO in charge. On one occasion, he accused members of stealing a pen from his desk. He interviewed all personnel and demanded the return of his stolen item. It was eventually located in his pocket. From time to time, he mumbled to himself, and he flew into unpredictable rages. When I arrived on the scene, he was extremely resentful of what he termed interference. After my first managerial review of his operation, he responded defensively to my findings, refusing to accept any responsibility for his actions and submitting a 22-page grievance alleging harassment and unfair treatment. The document was the *coup de grace* for this unfortunate individual, as it proved his unhinged state. Even though he initially resisted my findings, he eventually expressed his gratitude for the assistance he was given in his decision to retire and seek professional assistance. A competent commander replaced him and worked quickly to restore order and confidence at the detachment.

My second challenge involved a supervisor with ample inter-personal skills. The fundamental problem was his inexperience in managing a multifaceted operation. Because of the lack of monitoring, he had received little or no feedback from supervisors from the larger subdivision. RCMP detachments function under a complex diary system that requires members to update their progress on all investiga-tions by a specified date. An examination of this detachment revealed an inordinate number of overdue investigations. Although efforts were made to bring the detachment commander up to speed, he had attained sufficient service to retire to pension and decided to exercise that option. It took almost a year and two successive commanders to rectify all the outstanding issues at this detachment. The neglect of these two units clearly pointed to the necessity of reducing the size and complexity of the former subdivision.

One of Assistant Commissioner Henry's many skills was adopting effective strategies used elsewhere. Upon returning to an operational setting, I decided to wear a sidearm when on duty. Although this option was exercised in large detachments in British Columbia, offi-cers in the Prairies did not wear sidearms. As I travelled constantly on district roads alone and in uniform, I felt it prudent to be prepared to assist and engage if necessary. While visiting Division Headquarters, Henry questioned my rationale for wearing a sidearm. I explained why and told him that members in the field appeared to appreciate the ges-ture. I also told him I had participated in night patrol with detachment members when I was conducting my annual reviews. This idea had come to me after recalling my early days as a constable and the many personal discussions between members on night patrol. I observed that while my presence on these patrols was occasionally greeted with surprise and even uneasiness, the information I gleaned while riding shotgun in a patrol vehicle made it worthwhile. Most members quickly forgot they were riding with their officer commanding; as a result, they often expressed their true feelings. Not long after my conversation with Henry, he retired from the RCMP and assumed command of the Winnipeg City Police. Shortly after assuming his new position, the new chief was captured on local television in the company of a city police constable, wearing sidearms while conducting a bar check. The impact on both the citizenry and the city police was extremely positive, as a chief had never before been observed under such operational circumstances.

After establishing the subdivision office and bringing the two largest operations up to standard, I turned my attention to other administrative duties. As I would not have an assistant NCO, I knew I had to secure the services of a capable secretary. Lorna Lawson, a local woman with previous RCMP experience, won the competition. She became clerk, secretary, personnel officer, section NCO, chaplain, social convener and receptionist, in addition to being girl Friday. She also found time to introduce me to the woman who would become my wife. Lynne was a nursing instructor in Winnipeg who fulfilled all my hopes and dreams of a life mate. We were married in our backyard in Carman, with Lorna proudly looking on.

Lorna very capably ran the subdivision office and coordinated my movements, allowing me to remain on the road. Like most detachment stenographers employed from coast to coast to coast, Lorna was the mortar that held the bricks of the organization together. She remained in her position long after I departed, performing wonderful work and providing continuity between subdivision commanders. I will be forever indebted to her loyalty and her dedication.

WHILE POSTED IN Manitoba, I became involved in a conflict originating in a Hutterite colony. The Hutterite people have lived on the Prairies since the turn of the 20th century, when they settled on large tracts of land in the Canadian west. A communal religious sect, they

BE CAREFUL WHAT YOU WISH FOR ————————————

When I first married Lynne, she knew very little about the inner workings of the RCMP. It was an interesting learning curve for her, and she was bemused at the manner in which members of my command deferred to me, addressing me as "Sir" or calling me by my rank. I spent some time explaining the hierarchy to my new wife. With tongue in cheek, I told her that it would be appropriate for her to call me by my first name in private, but when in the company of other members she should address me as "Sir." She stared at me briefly in amazement, then realized the subtle tug on her leg. In retort, she assured me that she would be calling me "Sir" on appropriate occasions. However, I was to be clear that when she called me "Sir," it meant "shithead."

I paid dearly in years to come. Whenever we were in RCMP company, either socially or professionally, she would take every opportunity to call me "Sir," knowing full well that she was giving me a cruel jab.

———————————————————————————————

exemplified how people could live in harmony and forgo many of the frivolous trappings of North American society. They are extremely law abiding and good citizens, though they lead a rather closed existence. Hard-working and successful farmers, they take advantage of bulk purchasing to buy tractors, trucks and farm implements at substantial discounts. Everything is owned by the colony. For many years the system has functioned effectively, allowing Hutterite colonies to expand and prosper; however, during my tenure in Carman subdivision, rifts were beginning to appear within some colonies.

I'd had contact with the Hutterites over the years, as the colonies were always great places to buy produce, but I had seldom dealt with them from a police perspective. One of the largest colonies fell under my purview, and I received a visit from the leader. He told me that he had attended the detachment responsible for his colony, demanding they take action against a thief. The detachment commander had deemed the incident civil in nature and said no police action could be taken. When I asked him to describe the details of the alleged theft, he explained that one of his sons had left the colony, taking a truck and two tractors worth over $1 million. I asked him who had title to the vehicles, and he said they were part of the colony and accordingly owned by all. His son was still considered part of the sect even though he had left the colony. When I outlined the problem of determining ownership of the vehicles, the colony's leader refused to recognize that the matter was of a civil nature and not criminal. Unaccustomed to having his authority challenged, he became angry and assured me that he would carry his complaint beyond my level. Travelling immediately to Winnipeg, where Division Headquarters was located, he demanded action from the commanding officer. After receiving a response identical to mine, he voiced his displeasure to the commissioner of the RCMP and the attorney general of the province.

The dilemma culminated in one of the largest and lengthiest civil hearings in Manitoba history; however, the decisions of the court resolved little, as true ownership of communal property was almost impossible to identify. Many Hutterite colonies were experiencing similar fragmentation. Some young colony members, disillusioned with a conservative lifestyle based on religious beliefs, had begun to rebel. They were leaving the colonies and seeking their share of communal holdings. This dispute carried on for years with little or no resolution, and to my knowledge these intra-family conflicts have not been finally resolved.

The initial complaint from the Hutterite leader to the police exemplifies the dilemma faced by law-enforcement agencies. Many civil disputes cannot be solved by police intervention, yet police are still bound to keep the peace between dissenting parties. Police frequently find themselves intervening when physical confrontations result. Some Hutterite colony disputes have resulted in conflict exacerbated by the presence of firearms.

Working in small prairie communities, I rarely rubbed elbows with the criminal elite, but my rural routine was interrupted when senior management informed me that I would be the officer overseeing an operation involving a group of high-profile Hells Angels. The chapter presidents of this infamous outlaw biker gang were gathering in Winnipeg, and these crown princes of mayhem planned to take a ceremonial motorcycle ride along the Trans-Canada Highway. Their custom bikes, many valued in excess of $30,000, were flown into Winnipeg from Europe, Britain and the USA. As they gathered at the most expensive Winnipeg hotels, the RCMP and local police forces conducted surveillance. We intended to intercept the group just west of the city in order to fly the flag, establish control and generally show our authority. As the operations commander, I had at my disposal an arrest team, an investigational team and a heavily armed emergency response team. The Identification section would also be on hand to take photos and videos of the group.

In anticipation of the arrival of the motorcycles, we were positioned at a provincial weigh scale just east of Winnipeg, adjacent to Highway No. 1. As expected, the 40 Hells Angels presidents rode up astride their iron horses. They had been advised of our intent and obediently pulled onto the parking area, at which time I informed the lead rider of our purpose. The tension was palpable, but seeing the level of armament and personnel on site, the outlaws knew they were vulnerable. They had taken great care to avoid carrying any illicit items that would give grounds for a search. Their opulence and wealth was made evident by the display of Rolex watches, heavy gold chains, diamond jewellery and, of course, very expensive bikes. Video cameras were hard at work, operated by police, bikers and interested media. The emergency response team assumed strategic locations surrounding the group, automatic weapons at the ready. Some minor traffic tickets were issued, but little in the way of criminality was detected. After an hour of tense confrontation, the cavalcade was permitted to continue, minus two motorcycles that failed to meet the safety requirements of the Highway Traffic Act. As they moved down the highway, it was clear that they were among those in our world who profit from flaunting many of society's laws with impunity.

LIFE AS THE commander of the Carman subdivision was pretty close to idyllic. The communities were welcoming and supportive, crime was routinely minor, and after addressing initial concerns I had few personnel problems to deal with. But although I enjoyed my work there immensely, I was disillusioned with life in the upper echelon of my beloved Force. The prerequisites for upward mobility in the RCMP were readily apparent. One had to have a compliant demeanour, frequent the officer's mess, become fluently bilingual and remain at the ready to serve anywhere the commissioner decreed. The casual camaraderie and closeness that was so valued amongst NCOs, and especially constables, was largely absent in the officer ranks. Even though the line between commissioned and non-commissioned members had become slightly blurred, I was uncomfortable with the elitist mindset that dominated the upper strata of the RCMP.

It was time to contemplate the balance of my career and my life to determine what was intrinsically important. I had long desired to live on Vancouver Island, where I had spent some of my youth, and Lynne and I planned to move there eventually. In 1988, while on a holiday to visit my parents in Victoria, Lynne and I travelled to Courtenay, a Vancouver Island community north of the provincial capital. We purchased a beautiful oceanview lot and made plans to build our ideal home. We returned to the Prairies, hoping that our dream of watching the sunsets over the Pacific Ocean might become reality.

CHAPTER 14

HOME AT LAST

Not long after Lynne and I returned to Carman from our BC holiday, I learned that the assistant officer commanding of Courtenay subdivision was requesting a transfer. I immediately contacted a former colleague who was in charge of commissioned officer postings in Ottawa, alerting him of my interest in the position. These personal requests seldom get a positive response, and I held out faint hope. I had started to consider possible business opportunities and jobs outside the Force that would allow me to relocate to Courtenay so was amazed when I received a call asking if I was still interested in the position. I felt like I had won the lottery. We arrived in Courtenay in the spring of 1989. Our new home was waiting, built on our half-acre of wooded land, overlooking the Strait of Georgia. We felt we had reached the pinnacle of our lives.

The Courtenay subdivision was a mammoth operation consisting of 350 personnel, 16 detachments, a number of plainclothes units, a dog section and a helicopter. To round out the complement, two 60-foot patrol vessels, which could be used as floating detachments when needed, were strategically placed on each side of Vancouver Island. Police personnel who arrive in British Columbia after serving in

WELCOME TO BRITISH COLUMBIA?

Just prior to my transfer from Carman, Manitoba, to Courtenay, British Columbia, my new commanding officer, Deputy Commissioner Don Wilson, phoned to invite me to the annual COs' conference in Vancouver. The conference was a large gathering of all commissioned officers in the province, and discussions revolved around a "state of the union" address from the CO and his administrative officers. The assembly took place in "E" Division Headquarters with about 100 personnel present.

Being a new arrival, I felt somewhat on edge. As I entered the room, the CO spotted me and introduced himself. We had a brief chat and made our way over to the coffee urn, where I offered to buy the CO his coffee. He accepted and then made his way around the room. I realized at the time that I was being watched by a dour-looking soul. He made his way over to where I was standing.

"You're Parsons from Manitoba, are you not?" he asked accusingly. When I replied in the affirmative, he jumped right into the matter that was bothering him. "You just bought the CO coffee, did you not?" I stammered slightly telling him so. By now he was visibly agitated. "That's my job, Parsons, and don't think you can barge in here from Manitoba and take over!" He spun on his heel and stomped off as I stood there astounded. An old friend of mine who had been watching the encounter came up to me laughing and informed me I had just been taken in by Superintendent Cam Munro, a legend in the division for his pranks. Others told me that Cam had trouble controlling his laughter as he had turned away from me. A fine welcome to my new division! I later learned that Cam was extremely affable and one of the best-liked officers in the province, but that didn't help my initial shock.

---

other parts of Canada experience what can only be described as culture shock. The intensity and complexity of police operations in Canada's westernmost province cannot be compared to any other RCMP operation. Members serving in all but BC's most isolated detachments encounter a much greater intensity of crime. Consequently, employee burnout and stress-related problems in BC far exceed that experienced in other provinces.

Due to my experience working in rural detachments in other parts of Canada, I expected to take a hands-on role. When a relatively serious event occurs after hours in most places in rural Canada, the detachment commander is roused and advised. The first priority of the investigating member is to inform the man in charge. Consequently, my instructions to members had always been to call and advise, day or night. Reaching out from a deep sleep to grope for a ringing phone was part of the job. The officer commanding in Courtenay subdivision also had a prairie policing background and felt he should be told about serious incidents. It was clearly a shock to us when we arrived at our office on a Monday morning to discover there had been murders, rapes, assaults and an assortment of additional serious offences that we were unaware of. During the acculturation process, our senior NCOs assured us that this was the way things were done in BC. Many larger detachments had their own serious-crime, identification and police-dog units, enabling them to act autonomously. The sheer volume of crime precluded advising subdivision unless unique circumstances compelled additional resources. Initially, the approach was unsettling, but it quickly became evident that matters were handled quite differently in British Columbia, and the mechanisms of handling heavy crime loads were tried and true.

I also observed another interesting phenomenon. There were far fewer British Columbia senior NCOs entering the officer candidate program than those entering from other provinces. British Columbia has by far the largest concentration of RCMP members in Canada, including many very capable senior members who would excel in the officer candidate program. The anomaly was clearly attributable to the reluctance of most BC members to leave the province. Entering the officer candidate program requires mobility across Canada, and traditionally the Force has not permitted newly commissioned officers to serve in the province from whence they came. Recently, this policy has been modified, which has encouraged more members from British Columbia to participate in the officer candidate program.

North and central Vancouver Island is home to a rich tapestry of First Nations, many of which have occupied the same location for thousands of years. Their cultures—customs, art and traditions—were complex, sophisticated and deeply enhanced by the permanence of their settlements, the abundance of local food and moderate temperatures. This contrasted with the lifestyles of First Nations of the Prairies whom I had formerly worked with, who were nomadic by necessity. At the time I arrived, RCMP members had inadequate cultural awareness of Native peoples and communication with them was poor. In fact, Bob Gillen, the senior crown prosecutor based in Victoria, was so concerned about how the aboriginal community in northern Vancouver Island regarded the justice system that he proposed a committee to study the issue.

The committee comprised Mr. Gillen, a provincial judge, representatives from social services and probation and me, as RCMP representative. Our mission was to travel to various Native communities to conduct town hall–style meetings. One of the first meetings occurred on Cormorant Island, where the village of Alert Bay is situated. Our committee assembled in the local band hall, filled to capacity with villagers. I sensed quickly that the mood in the hall was less than hospitable. Shortly after Mr. Gillen introduced our panel, participants became vocal and abusive, and the meeting seemed on the brink of pandemonium. Just when I began to contemplate how I was going to safely extract the visiting dignitaries, a powerful-looking aboriginal man in the front row stood up and roared, "Quiet!" Obviously, this individual carried considerable influence with the citizens, as the noise quickly subsided. He addressed the throng, reminding them that the committee had come to the community to hear their concerns. He told the audience that he understood their frustrations, but there was no point in attacking those who were trying to resolve some of the problems. When he concluded, the audience took a more civil approach, though many complaints and concerns regarding the justice system were vented. I learned that our saviour was Bill Wilson, a noted Vancouver Island aboriginal leader and practising lawyer. Bill and I crossed paths many times in the years to follow, and we became friends. His sometimes surly reputation was well earned. He opened an address to members of the BC Bar Association in Vancouver by stating, "We should have killed you all!" Such statements certainly rewarded him with rapt attention from his listeners but also attracted negative publicity. I never knew him as an adversary, and he was always a positive mentor to me in my dealings with aboriginal people.

Native leaders on Vancouver Island made it clear that they harboured much residual bitterness as a result of mistakes made by governments of years past. Native residential schools and the suppression of the potlatch and other cultural practices stood at the top of the list of grievances. During a session that included RCMP members and First Nations people, I made the error of encouraging the Native participants not to look back, but to look forward and guide us in how we could improve our service to them. Basil Amber, a powerful presence and respected elder, rose up and bellowed his disagreement. In no uncertain terms, he instructed me to listen and not tell the people what I wanted them to do. I quickly concluded that it was not a good time to debate the issue, so we listened for hours about the injustices and cruelty foisted on aboriginal peoples by white society in years past.

Every session started in a similar fashion, and during breaks members would come and ask me why we had to listen to tales of long ago. I told them to be patient. Even though they were initially defensive, the members learned much about First Nations culture and developed empathy for what these people had suffered. As each three-day session progressed, it moved into discussions of what police could now do to improve relations. The members' willingness to sit and hear grievances was exactly what was needed. The sessions concluded with a wonderful traditional feast put on by the band. Many RCMP members, spouses and children participated and left with changed attitudes and a much greater understanding of First Nations people and culture. Yet despite all the steps taken to improve the RCMP's attitude toward Native people, I was troubled to see that some senior personnel still harboured prejudice and dislike for them. No amount of positive interaction with Native people seemed to change their entrenched opinions.

Even with my long experience with First Nations, both in the field and in the classroom, I had more to learn. While formulating course material, I commented to some members of a north island nation that another nation to the south and west of them had introduced a series of cross-cultural experiences for the police that had been very successful. Sensing a cool reception, I asked one of the elders why my suggestion was not looked upon with favour. The elder told me that the Native group I mentioned was traditionally an enemy of the northern people, and communication between the two groups was minimal. Any suggestion that ideas from the south be implemented was clearly inappropriate. The following day I made amends and assured them that adopting ideas from other groups would not be an option. This seemed to satisfy the participants, and we went on to design a course almost identical to the one being employed to the south.

The troubling case of Roy Hunter demonstrated how the unwieldy RCMP bureaucracy more often than not overrode important local policies and ideas. Roy was a Native special constable attached to the Alert Bay detachment on Cormorant Island, just east of the northern end of Vancouver Island. The culturally intricate community had always been a challenge to police, and Roy had contributed much to the RCMP operation there for 17 years. In 1994, a woman in her 30s disclosed to a social worker that she and Roy had been sexually intimate when she was 15 years old, and she had been guilt-ridden since that time. Roy had been 16 when the sexual activity had allegedly occurred. The social worker relayed the information to the detachment commander, and an investigation was commenced. Roy readily admitted to being involved, but in view of the tender age of both parties, the prosecutor, the police and the community concurred that the case might be handled via aboriginal justice and a sentencing circle of elders. The complainant was also in agreement with this alternative. Earlier in 1994, Commissioner Norman Inkster had issued a no-tolerance policy for any RCMP member involved in a sexual offence. Perpetrators would be dismissed forthwith. However, Roy's case had been discussed within "E" Division British Columbia, and it had been agreed that we would proceed by way of aboriginal justice. Special Constable Hunter appeared before the elders, where an apology to the victim was ordered along with some community constraints for a period of time. Everyone involved seemed satisfied with the action taken.

A couple of weeks after the aboriginal hearing, a directive from HQ Ottawa arrived, ordering Constable Hunter's immediate dismissal. I was to go to Alert Bay, inform him of this decision and obtain his RCMP revolver, his warrant of appointment and his badge. We tried to countermand the order but were summarily commanded to proceed. It was one of the longest helicopter flights I had ever taken. Constable Hunter was waiting for my arrival and had no idea of the purpose of my visit. He later told me when I asked for his badge and his gun, his entire world collapsed. As I returned to Courtenay, many thoughts ran through my mind, including offering my resignation. I was seeing more and more irrational decisions that were adversely affecting members. Senior management regarded officers as part of the problem and made decisions with no input from us. In addition to the trauma Constable Hunter endured, it also lowered public regard for the Force in Alert Bay. Shortly after this incident, I did decide to retire. While Hunter's dismissal was not the only reason for my decision, it did leave a bad taste in my mouth.

I later learned that one of the division staff relations representatives whom RCMP members appointed to act on behalf of members with grievances had taken up Constable Hunter's case and instigated an appeals process. It took two years and several boards, but the decision against Hunter was reversed and he was reinstated. When he was phoned about this news, his wife answered, as Roy was not home. The party disclosed the news of the reinstatement and told his wife to pass it along. It was an unnecessarily terse communication from management to someone who had been waiting for this decision for months. Constable Hunter relocated to Port Hardy at the north end of Vancouver Island and returned to serving his people, the RCMP and Canada.

My travels to meet with First Nations people or visit outlying detachments took me to many locations in northern Vancouver Island and the adjacent smaller islands—surely the most spectacular setting in all of Canada, if not North America. Many of our detachments were located on coastal islands or on the edge of remote areas of the mainland that could only be reached by ferry or helicopter. I had purchased a cruising boat for my own enjoyment and would occasionally use it to travel to detachments, where I conducted inspections and interviewed members. Travelling in this manner also allowed me to visit isolated villages and evaluate community satisfaction with the RCMP. During my off-duty time, I often went salmon fishing.

The largely unpopulated wilderness of the West Coast has long been attractive to marijuana growers. Two major drug busts occurred during my tenure on Vancouver Island, and both indicated to me that the war on drugs long waged in both Canada and the United States was being lost. A sophisticated grow operation was discovered on a remote island in a pristine area called Desolation Sound. Anything but desolate, it is an ocean paradise frequented by pleasure boaters from all over the world. It is vast, with mountainous terrain, and only accessible by boat or plane. Although the waters of the sound are frequently travelled, the coast and islands are virtually uninhabited. Police regularly fly over the entire area, looking for the distinctive green that identifies marijuana plants. In many areas, the natural vegetation is so dense that discerning marijuana grow ops is a challenging task. Such was the case on an island in Desolation Sound.

REGIMENTAL ELK

Gold River is a picturesque community west of Campbell River at the head of Muchalat Inlet. In 1990, Corporal John Ollinger was the detachment commander supervising two constables. Christmas was looming and they were trying to design a unique greeting card that would represent the detachment. On the highway leading into Gold River there is a spectacular wooden elk, easily 20 feet high and with a majestic set of antlers. It is a stunning sight and very realistic except for its exaggerated dimensions. The three innovative guardians of the law decided that this elk should figure in their Christmas card. When Christmas rolled around we received our annual greetings from the boys in Gold River. When we opened the card, all we could do was gasp. There, seated one behind the other on the back of the elk, were the three members of Gold River detachment, clad in red serge. They had used an extension ladder to climb up onto the elk for the picture. Of course, they sent the card all over the country, including to Division Headquarters in Vancouver. The response from Vancouver was less than enthusiastic. They called it frivolous and unprofessional. We called it the RCMP Christmas card of the decade.

A woman disclosed that her unfaithful lover was involved in a major illicit marijuana operation, even describing its location. With the assistance of one of the police patrol catamarans and an emergency response team, the drug squad swooped down on the island. Even when on top of the location, it was virtually impossible to determine its scope. Eventually, a hothouse almost half the size of a football field was discovered. It was illuminated with artificial light supplied by commercial-sized generators and irrigated by an automatic system. The building was ingeniously camouflaged and built around gigantic Douglas firs, making it completely invisible from the air. Thousands of juvenile and mature marijuana plants were thriving under careful nurturing. As there was no one present at the scene, we hid all evidence of our presence and awaited the arrival of the amateur botanists. After a while, a large vessel appeared, ostensibly to take on a load of marijuana.

The men aboard were arrested, and the vessel and all paraphernalia were seized. It was impossible to determine how long the operation had been in existence or how many marijuana crops had been taken off in the past. It was estimated that a single crop would generate $9 million on the street. A small helicopter was also seized and several individuals were charged under the Narcotic Control Act.

Another major drug case occurred in Courtenay. A concerned citizen reported strange comings and goings in a neighbouring home. Large cube vans were arriving late at night and unloading unidentifiable cargo into an outbuilding next to the residence. As the activity had been going on for some weeks, the drug squad set up surveillance. Over a period of time, they found that the initial cargo was being off-loaded at a small ocean cove on the west coast of Vancouver Island and transported to a residence. One of the van drivers was identified as someone who had previously been involved in drug trafficking. A search warrant was obtained for the suspicious building, and one night, when delivery activity was at its peak, the drug squad, backed up by the emergency response team, descended. Another well-organized operation was discovered, along with two tons of hashish, valued at millions of dollars. The bales of hashish had obviously come from a mother-ship operation that moved drugs from Mexico up the coast and delivered them to remote locations. Once at the destination, the material was packed into tidy wooden crates professionally labelled "BC Fish Product" and loaded back into the vans for shipping to eastern Canada and the USA.

Once again, several were charged under the Narcotic Control Act. The drugs were ordered destroyed, which presented a logistical problem since a large commercial furnace was needed to efficiently dispose of the huge volume of hashish. We made arrangements with a pulp mill to use their blast furnaces for the purpose. When burning day arrived, the drugs were transported via truck, accompanied once again by the drug squad and emergency response team. With security at a high level, members carried out the demanding physical task of heaving the hashish bales into the furnace. Great plumes of white smoke rose from the stacks as many of the workers stood by, mourning all the highs that were not to be. That particular afternoon, as the seagulls swooped over the mill, we wondered what kind of psychedelic trips they might be experiencing.

Both of these major drug operations would have gone undetected had citizens not passed on information to the police, which makes me wonder how many others operate with impunity. In spite of millions of dollars and untold manpower hours expended by law enforcement, illegal drug activity continues growing at an unprecedented rate. It is difficult not to make comparisons with the prohibition of alcohol in the 1920s and '30s. When alcohol was interdicted, it was forced underground, creating a perfect environment for organized crime to flourish. In addition to the loss of revenue through taxation, governments devoted immeasurable law-enforcement resources to banishing the manufacture, sale and transport of alcohol. When they realized the futility of the process, prohibition was repealed and the production and sale of alcohol was again legalized and taxed. The money and manpower expended on the drug war dwarfs that spent enforcing prohibition, yet law makers fail to see history repeating itself.

Rex Forteau was one of the most successful northern Vancouver Island drug traffickers. Try as they might, the drug squad seemed incapable of nabbing him. Because he was Metis and had such great success eluding prosecution, the local Natives believed he was a shaman who could not be harmed. Forteau's profits allowed him to live a life of opulence. He owned a large property just outside the city of Campbell River, countless boats and vehicles and a resort in the BC Interior. Women were at his beck and call. It was almost as if the RCMP had given up on him, as he brazenly continued to ply his business without interference, likely raking in millions of dollars.

Forteau's only mistake was the company he kept. He frequently associated with Mike Flynn, locally known as a boozer and a cokehead with a monumentally bad temper, especially when he was drunk or high. Forteau and Flynn had picked up a couple of girls, and with George Foot, another associate, drove out into the boonies to have a party. While they were parked on a remote logging road south of Campbell River, Flynn got into an argument with one of the girls. He slapped her, and the other girl tried to intervene. Both girls were seated in the back seat of the vehicle with Foot. Enraged, Flynn pulled out a revolver and shot both girls, killing them instantly. Foot, terrified by what he had seen, dove out of the vehicle and ran into the bush. When the girls failed to return home, their families registered missing-persons' reports with the Campbell River detachment. Several weeks later, a hiker stumbled onto the shallow gravesites of the two girls and immediately called the RCMP. Detectives soon traced the girls' last movements, learning that they had been in the company of Forteau, Flynn and Foot at a bar in Campbell River the night they went missing. There was no sign of Forteau or Flynn, but Foot was located and brought in for questioning. When confronted, he became extremely upset and blurted out the complete story.

The RCMP was now hot on the trail of Forteau and Flynn and determined they were hiding out at Forteau's resort at Babine Lake in central northern BC. They were arrested and brought back to Campbell River to stand trial on two counts of first-degree murder. Once again, it appeared as though Forteau was leading a charmed life. He claimed to be only a witness to the murders, even though it was known he assisted in disposing of the bodies. In spite of Crown objections, Forteau was released on bail, though Flynn was held in custody. However, inexorably, it began to appear that Forteau was no longer invulnerable. One of the murdered girl's brothers was an affiliate of the Hells Angels chapter in Nanaimo, BC. Unconfirmed intelligence indicated the brother approached the Hells Angels for some assistance in the matter, and possibly revenge.

Prior to his upcoming trial, Forteau was relaxing in his country estate, watching his giant television in his sumptuous living room. The home was alarmed, and the entire property was surveyed by video cameras. While Forteau and his lady sat in the living room, visible through the large picture window, they were mowed down by what was determined to be a .45 calibre machine gun. Forteau died instantly, and his partner was crippled for life. Mysteriously, the alarms and video cameras were not working on the night of the murder. The investigation into Rex Forteau's murder is ongoing to this day, and the Native people no longer consider him a shaman. Mike Flynn was convicted of two counts of first-degree murder.

A TRAGIC MURDER that occurred in Courtenay demonstrated clearly the dedication, work ethic, skills and knowledge of younger members. The strangled body of a six-year-old girl was found at the edge of a forested area adjacent to some apartment buildings. The murder of a child throws a community into a state of fear and panic. National and local media shone their glaring lights upon us, and the pressure to determine who was responsible was intense. Investigators worked 24/7 to solve the terrible crime, a good part of that time being voluntary. The eventual encounter with the troubled, youthful killer was a classic example of top-calibre investigational and interrogation techniques. The processing of the scene and all evidence was precise and meticulous. The accused was arrested and eventually convicted and sentenced to life in prison, where he later committed suicide. The case proved to me that the expertise of modern RCMP investigators matches and even surpasses that of previous generations.

Two aspects of my duties on Vancouver Island were new to me. First, I became an emergency response team (ERT) commander. In addition to their routine duties, the dedicated members of the ERT are on call 24/7 to respond to any and all situations requiring expertise in unconventional arrests at sea and on land, weaponry, hostage taking

WAS IT JOE PARSONS'S LUCK?

In 1994 I learned that a newly arrived junior member to Courtenay detachment had just received an award for scoring the highest mark ever recorded on a Recruit Field Training exam. Thinking this a rather special accomplishment, I called the young member and his trainer up to my office. I had a spare pair of old-style RCMP collar badges, or "dogs" as they are known in the trade, that had been issued to my father, Joe Parsons, who wore them throughout his service. I had inherited them and worn them in turn. They are quite rare and much coveted within the Force. I congratulated the young member and presented him with the collar dogs.

I retired later that year and time marched on. One of my recruits, Guiliano Zaccardelli, was appointed commissioner. The first woman commissioner, Beverley Busson, replaced Zaccardelli on an interim basis. When she stepped down, William Elliott, the first civilian commissioner, took the reins. It was a time of chaos and scandals for the Force. When Elliott resigned, there was a careful search for the next commissioner, who was expected to bring the Force into the 21st century. When the announcement was made, the name of the new commissioner was vaguely familiar. I sent him an email asking if he was the young constable to whom I had presented the collar dogs in Courtenay. Commissioner Bob Paulson replied that he was in fact that person, and he wore the badges proudly on his dress uniform. I told him that somewhere up there Joe Parsons was looking down with a big grin on his face, knowing that at least his collar badges made it to the highest office in the RCMP.

---

or barricaded persons—virtually anything that takes specialized law-enforcement skills. The ERT consists of a commander, negotiator, police service dog and several sharpshooters. In the case of a hostage taking or barricaded person, once the team is in place, it is the negotiator's job to make contact with the perpetrator in an attempt to establish rapport. The ultimate decision to continue negotiations, assault the premises or shoot the suspect rests with the commander. Such situations can and do end with fatalities, so the assistance of the ERT is always welcomed by uniformed detachment members encountering these tense situations.

Environmental protests were a regular occurrence on Vancouver Island, an area heavily dependent on the forest industry. My first encounter with protesters was on the Tsitika River basin near Telegraph Cove on northern Vancouver Island. A group of people had chained themselves to large pieces of logging equipment in an attempt to obstruct logging operations. The logging company filed injunctions that permitted the RCMP to intervene and make arrests if necessary. Arrest teams were assembled, pulling detachment and highway patrol members away from their demanding daily routines. During these protests, we boarded a chartered bus every morning at 4:00 a.m. for the three-hour trip to the protest site. On almost every occasion, Corporal Grant Wyton and his emergency response team accompanied the contingent.

Corporal Wyton never received the recognition he deserved. A tough, resourceful, resolute man, he kept himself in peak physical condition. On one occasion on the Tsitika River, a protester scaled a 200-foot Douglas fir, making it hazardous to commence logging operations nearby. When ERT members tried to scale the tree, the protester dropped containers of urine on them. Ever the innovator, Corporal Wyton enlisted the services of a tree faller. He explained to the protester in the tree that he would be given 10 minutes to descend from his perch. If there was no response, the tree would be cut down. The 10 minutes expired with no reaction from the protester, so Corporal Wyton instructed the faller to start his chainsaw and cut into an adjacent tree. The climber, of course, assumed it was his tree and scampered down to be arrested.

During the '90s, the protests reached their pinnacle on the west coast of Vancouver Island at Clayoquot Sound, cherished by environmentalists for its old-growth forests. Tensions between protesters and the logging industry had gradually escalated to a fever pitch, and protesters had chained themselves to logging equipment. RCMP members were detailed as arrest teams to preserve the peace and intervene between the two sides. It was the duty of the RCMP to first advise protesters of a court order demanding they cease and desist interfering with forestry workers. Once the order was read, the protesters were vulnerable to arrest. As the confrontation gathered momentum, worldwide media were on hand with cameras to record every move. The tension between police, loggers and protesters was palpable. It was an extremely delicate balance; the police needed to ensure the appearance of impartiality, yet clear the area of protesters. Every move was recorded by countless video cameras. During these confrontations, some protesters went to great lengths to goad police into overstepping the bounds of reasonable force.

Proactivity is one of the most valuable assets in law enforcement. Anticipating cause and effect can often assist in preventing tense situations from spiralling out of control. The team leaders coordinating the arrests were senior operational NCOs from regular law-enforcement duties. The manner in which these members accepted and discharged their particular duties under extreme pressure spoke volumes about their training, experience and professionalism. Several of these senior NCOs had accumulated many hours on protest lines up and down the BC coast, so they were well qualified to deal with such situations. One of them, Staff Sergeant Len Doyle, made a point of visiting the protest camp during his off-duty hours. He approached in civilian clothing as the protesters gathered around an evening bonfire. People from all walks of life huddled about, shrouded in clouds of marijuana smoke. Doyle assured the group he was not there in an official capacity and informed them he wished to discuss protest procedure for the following day. The protesters greeted him with skepticism, and many considered him the enemy, but his easy, confident manner lowered tensions. Doyle offered assurances of restraint by members if there were arrests. He explained the protesters would be granted their moment of fame in front of the cameras; following this they would be gently touched, arrested and moved off the line. This kind of dialogue greatly alleviated tensions between police and protesters, and as a result, arrests proceeded in an orderly, almost carnival-like manner.

During the Clayoquot Sound protests, almost 900 persons were arrested without a single injury to police or protesters. Interestingly, many of the arrestees took to wearing a T-shirt emblazoned with the phrase "Foiled by Doyle." It was the largest environmental protest in the history of Canada. In many countries, a similar event would have culminated in injuries and even death. Sole credit for the complete safety of citizens is attributable to the calmness and professionalism of all RCMP members. Staff Sergeant Doyle and his counterpart, Staff Sergeant Bernie Johnston, were recommended for Commissioner's Commendations for their outstanding performance under duress. Both of these capable NCOs had been instrumental in resolving almost all of the environmental protests up and down the BC coast. Although entirely deserving of the Commissioner's award, division management reduced the recommendation to the lesser Commanding Officer's Commendation.

During the Clayoquot protest, the Australian rock group Midnight Oil gave an impromptu concert to demonstrate support for the protesters and their cause. The show was attended by upwards of 3,000 people. Participants included members of the logging community, many of whom were angry and resentful that their livelihood was threatened by outsiders. With a complement of less than 20 officers, the RCMP preserved order and prevented the event from deteriorating into chaos and riot. This again was attributable to their calm demeanour and clear position of neutrality. One of the RCMP members almost went too far in exhibiting a spirit of cooperation, sneaking backstage to obtain autographs from the band. Although there were moments of confrontation in the crowd, RCMP members defused them instantly, preventing further escalation.

My long-held dream of living and working on the West Coast had been achieved. I had saved my favourite place for last and was ready to ease into retirement on beautiful Vancouver Island. But despite my love of the West Coast scenery, my most rewarding policing experiences came from my prairie postings. Prairie law enforcement involves many personal connections, primarily due to the rural nature of the area, and the RCMP has been a part of the social fibre of prairie communities for as long as the organization has existed.

Unlike in the Prairies, in British Columbia the Force was deployed in cities from the outset. Urban law enforcement is intense, complex and harrowing. A rookie constable may experience more in one year in the Lower Mainland of British Columbia than many prairie members encounter in a decade. Accordingly, there are more stress-related problems in BC, more mistakes and wrongdoing and less fond regard for the police.

Because of these difficult circumstances, RCMP detachments in BC have relied heavily on volunteers. Almost from its inception, the Force has distinguished between "regular" members and all others, which include detachment spouses, civilian members, clerical staff, auxiliary police, citizens on patrol (COPs) and Victim Services personnel. Although all of these people have contributed significantly in other provinces, they have been fundamental to the very survival of the RCMP in British Columbia. This is especially true of auxiliary police personnel, COPs and Victim Services.

In large British Columbia detachments, auxiliary constables almost always augment work shifts. These stalwarts are civilians who volunteer countless hours of service. They come from all walks of life and are motivated by civic pride and a wish to contribute to a healthier and more secure community. Auxiliary constables have always had to fight for their place in the RCMP, often only receiving appreciation and recognition from the detachment in which they serve. The bureaucracy in Ottawa has perennially discounted their value, more often than not perceiving them as an irritation, not an asset. Only recently have auxiliary constables been given dress uniforms and small tokens of appreciation for their service. Without the thousands of hours spent by auxiliary constables accompanying regular members and doing traffic and crowd control at major public functions, the RCMP could not meet its staffing requirements. There are numerous examples of senior auxiliary constables taking junior and newly arrived members under their wing, introducing them to the community and advising them of potential problems.

The other supporting players are equally valuable. COP is another volunteer group that donates services and vehicles to monitor the community and advise of potential or developing problem areas. Victim Services are a cadre of caregivers who stand by to offer counselling to victims of crime. And for more than a hundred years, RCMP members' spouses, traditionally wives, particularly in rural areas, have been invaluable in responding to incoming phone calls, acting as matrons during police escorts and performing daily tasks that could easily occupy the time of additional members. They can never be adequately reimbursed. Civilian members and special constables function as RCMP pilots, crime-detection specialists, analysts and resource persons, yet administrators have always thought of them as having only one foot in the canoe. Some organizations deal with employee inequity more effectively than others and strive to improve the working conditions of support people. The RCMP has not always done so.

FEW INCIDENTS ARE more traumatic than the disappearance of a child. Even the families of law-enforcement personnel are vulnerable to such a tragedy, and just months prior to my retirement the loss of a child was visited upon a recently arrived couple to our Courtenay operation. Their 14-year-old daughter had been a runaway from the family home in the Vancouver area. The couple had hoped the relocation to Courtenay would facilitate their reconciliation with the girl. Continuing problems with the child had resulted in her being placed in a foster residence near the new family home. In August of 1993, the daughter disappeared from this residence. In light of her history, there was no immediate panic, but the usual protocols for missing children were deployed. As the days turned to months, investigations became more intense, and anxiety over her welfare was very evident, not just on the part of investigators, but among the entire police community. In spite of all the efforts of heavily deployed police and community resources, the girl was never found. There were a number of members who felt a personal responsibility for their failure to discern the whereabouts of this RCMP dependant, and it clearly affected morale. Almost 20 years have passed, and no progress has been made in the case. The girl's mother, Judy Peterson, has become a tireless advocate for the formulation of a missing-persons and found-remains data bank for Canada.

AFTER FIVE YEARS' travelling and savouring the flavours of Vancouver Island, I decided to conclude my long and satisfying career. The Force had presented me with several tempting offers of promotion and relocation, but after reaching Vancouver Island at the most appropriate stage of my career, I had no intention of further uprooting Lynne, who had just completed her master's degree in nursing and was on the faculty of a local college, or Lynne's son, Adam, who was just completing high school. There was nothing more I wished to accomplish as a member of the Force. I had loved the ride and was ready to savour whatever was left. There were fond adieus but no sad farewells as I stepped out of harness into the next stage of my life.

When I was a young constable, I heard an accomplished veteran remark that it was far more stimulating to experience different regions and duties than to limit oneself to a single place or position. He went on to observe that too many police personnel have one year's service 35 times, rather than 35 years of interesting and varied challenges. I was fortunate that my career followed the latter course. While I had some say in directing my career, it was also steered by circumstance and good luck. It is said that when your organization begins to seem a stranger, it is time to leave. The Force I left only slightly resembled the iconic organization I had joined some 33 years before. Canada had changed in amazing ways, and the RCMP had been dragged kicking and screaming into the 21st century.

THE END OF A DYNASTY?

Like most veterans of the Force, I view the new RCMP with trepidation. It is clear that the stresses and pressures currently put to bear upon our federal police force are unlike any other in its history. For the first time, the RCMP is being viewed as an organization whose best days are perhaps behind it. Since the NWMP marched west in 1874, Canada's famous Force has epitomized much of what is admirable about the country. Robert Stead's collection of childhood memories, which vividly convey a sense of wonder, closes with a sense of foreboding.

THE SQUAD OF ONE

Robert J.C. Stead (Reprinted from the October 1942 *RCMP Quarterly*)

One of the highlights of my boyhood on the prairie was the summer evening when Corporal Snow, N.W.M.P., reversing the tradition of Lochinvar, rode out of the East to my father's homestead in Southern Manitoba. We saw the scarlet speck a mile or more away; gradually it took shape, and when the supple rider swung from his horse in our door-yard I thought I never had seen anything so magnificent.

Corporal Snow's mission was to arrange for the lodging and board of two constables and their horses on our farm. We were by no means an unruly lot, and it was no reflection upon us or our community that two policemen were being billeted on us. We lived close to the Dakota border, and a chain of police posts was being established along the international boundary. They were not designed to resist an American invasion, but to discourage the tendency of settlers to ignore the boundary altogether, especially with respect to those commodities which could be bought cheaper south of the Line. In the 1880's, of which I write, something approaching the ideal of free trade had been clandestinely achieved by the good people of Manitoba and Dakota.

Corporal Snow had no difficulty in completing his arrangements, and soon after two policemen, who shall remain unnamed, arrived to take up their duties. These duties were not particularly arduous; they consisted mainly of keeping posts east and west advised of a threatened visit by the inspector. This piece of public service was reciprocal, with posts east and west keeping them equally advised. An incidental duty was to patrol the Boundary Line once a week. As this invisible line between two great nations was quite unfenced and almost unmarked, the effectiveness of such a patrol in restraining the free trade sentiment of the settlers may be imagined. I can recall only one seizure being made. It consisted of several loads of fresh fish captured in good Canadian waters and being exported without permit. The constables had no difficulty in seizing the fish, but as they could not find a buyer, disposal of the illicit stock presented a problem. And fresh fish, like time and tide, are notoriously opposed to undue delay.

When not engaged in the above and associated duties, our policemen cultivated the social grace of story-telling. I admired the police; had I been a girl I would surely have said they were beautiful. With their scarlet tunics, their belts filled with threatening cartridge—rifle cartridges for long range work; .44 revolver bullets for the murderous hand-to-hand business—their dark blue trousers with the wide yellow stripe, and collar-box caps perched airily on their heads one inch above the left eyebrow, in beauty they seemed to me greater than all the lilies of the field, and in authority next only to the Queen. Small wonder their eight-year-old audience sat with mouth agape far into the night! It did not then occur to me that beings so divine could take liberties with the star-like chastity of Truth. Alas, that the passing years dissolve so many illusions!

It is interesting to surmise what Corporal Snow and Corporal Joe Parsons would think about today's RCMP. They would be astounded by the appearance of women in policing and even more shocked when they learned that there already had been a female commissioner. I suspect their reaction would not be favourable.

Their eyes would roll at the sight of the personal equipment and combat-like clothing donned by a patrolling member. Where are the spurs? Where are the boots? What happened to the unique brown jacket and that terribly impractical pea jacket? The utility belt worn by members would certainly have reminded my father of old Batman comics. The ability to communicate instantly might make them ask, "What happened to independence?" Of course, the salary would appear to them exorbitant, as would the excessive time off and benefits like overtime, and—God forbid—maternity and paternity leave. What happened to single men? How can the Force operate without a cadre of people they can send anywhere at any time? Where are the horses?

They would be mystified by the presence of personnel whose only job is to look after the welfare of serving members. And what happened to having to sign "Your Obedient Servant" on all reports?

The RCMP would appear cold and mechanized to them. Much of the personal, human component that they knew has been obliterated, and the speed, intensity and volume of criminal activity would overwhelm them. I believe they would look at one another and hurry off back to the early 20th century.

During the summer of 2010, I visited Head-Smashed-In Buffalo Jump, located near Fort Macleod in southwestern Alberta. It is a museum and monument dedicated to Canada's first peoples and a way of life that has long since disappeared. It is an impressive edifice, and in spite of the numbers of tourists who visit the site, it is also a spiritual place that every Canadian should see at least once. For at least 5,500 years, the Native people of the area hunted buffalo here. They approached the massive animals on foot and herded them toward the edge of a high cliff. They were stampeded at the last moment, so the momentum of the herd took the animals over to their deaths. The women and children waited at the bottom to butcher prime animals for their choice parts. The site was abandoned in the 19th century after European contact, and by the mid-1880s the buffalo had been hunted almost to extinction, largely by professional hunters. Today, the animal that sustained the First Nations people and dominated the prairie ecosystem for millennia has been reduced to a smattering of herds located in protected areas of western Canada.

As I peered at the cliff where untold numbers of buffalo were herded to their deaths, another icon of the Canadian west came to mind: the Royal Canadian Mounted Police. From my earliest childhood, this worthy and durable organization has been a fundamental building block of my life. As a family member from a younger generation, Constable Adam Giesbrecht, Lynne's son, embarks on his RCMP career, one would think his future would be assured, as the demise of the RCMP seems as unlikely as did the disappearance of the plains buffalo, one of the symbols of the RCMP. However, perhaps there is an ominous similarity between the buffalo and the RCMP. Once the buffalo were pointed in the direction of the cliff, the run was commenced. The momentum was so great that nothing could prevent their rush over the precipice. Like the buffalo, the RCMP seem to be heading for the cliff. Momentum is building, and they soon may be over the edge.

How could this happen? What is precipitating this potential tragedy? The main reason is clear: a growing population and the increasing complexity of Canadian society have overwhelmed our frontier police force. Historically, when Corporal Snow patrolled in southern Manitoba, the Force accepted and discharged all facets of policing in the Canadian west. No matter what the request, this versatile body of men—now men and women—accepted the task and usually carried it out successfully. The mindset of the Mounted Police has always been "Never say 'no'" Even if the task overburdened the troops, the job was undertaken without question, and every effort was expended to meet challenges. This was the case when the RCMP expanded municipal responsibilities from small prairie communities to large cities after taking over provincial policing in BC. In the early 1950s, the RCMP began policing the municipality of Burnaby, BC, the first of several very large municipal details in the Lower Mainland. The logistics of supplying human resources for these operations were extremely taxing and sapped the Force in many other areas. Learning the trade of "big city policing" has been a long and difficult road, and many operations still run shorthanded in an effort to feed the monster consuming human resources in southern British Columbia.

As Canada began the transition to a multicultural society and the country's population increased, more cracks and fissures began to appear. The basic paramilitary infrastructure of the Force did not change, and the RCMP continued to be responsible for all levels of policing from coast to coast. Provincial contracts demanded more and more resources, as did growing municipal contracts. Our frontier police force continued to strive to be all things to all people in what was becoming a very diversified country.

RCMP administrators were loath to lobby governments to increase resources and generally tried to deal with inadequacies internally. During the 20th century, the Force operated on a shoestring. Most of the commissioners of the day prided themselves on coming in under budget at the conclusion of the fiscal year. The Force was perennially held up as an organization that functioned economically. This parsimony was, of course, at the cost of individual members. Salaries were dismal and reimbursement of on-the-job expenses was almost unheard of. Working conditions—police buildings and vehicles— were always basic. Heaters in cars were only allowed as late as the '50s. Commercial radios of any kind were not allowed in police vehicles, and on the rare occasion that one would appear so equipped, the radio would be removed. Air conditioning was not installed in vehicles until the late '60s. Members on patrol in winter conditions did so in high leather boots with spurs that conducted the cold, and until the 1960s, the winter overcoat was an unlined pea jacket, virtually useless in forty below temperatures. The alternative was a large, bulky buffalo coat that rendered the wearer impotent in any situation that required agility. An organization that should have functioned with efficiency, effectiveness and economy largely ignored the first two important goals in the interest of the third.

As long as RCMP members worked overtime hours without pay, the Force was able to assume additional mandates with insufficient personnel. But when overtime compensation was introduced in 1976, detachment and unit commanders were forced to cope with finite human resource budgets. For the first time in the Force's history, investigations began to be prioritized. It became obvious that there were insufficient human resources to carry out mandated responsibilities.

The important and necessary addition of women to the RCMP,

beginning in 1974, necessitated the introduction of maternity leave; however, female members on leave were not replaced and each time a vacancy occurred on the worksite because of pregnancy, remaining personnel were required to work extra hours. This caused resentment, insults and innuendo directed toward women on the job and set the stage for further deterioration of morale and more instances of stress leave.

During the 1970s, the RCMP attempted to balance their overwhelming workloads with the additional responsibility for Canada's national security. This caused serious shortcomings. Perhaps for the first time, the RCMP was challenged and scrutinized by a civilian entity. The McDonald Commission was appointed by the federal government in 1977 to examine serious flaws in how the RCMP was functioning at the national security level. While the Force carried a mandate to detect political subversion within the country, this was done by an entity completely separate from the criminal investigation component. R.H. Simmonds, the commissioner of the day, closely monitored McDonald Commission activity to ensure it did not extend its tentacles into what was referred to as the Criminal Investigation Branch side of the Force. If it were not for his stewardship of the organization during this extremely stressful period, the Force might have found itself compromised beyond repair.

The commission examined and substantiated a number of allegations against the RCMP Security Service, including theft of a Parti Québécois membership list, break-ins, illegal opening of mail and the burning of a barn in Quebec where the FLQ (Front de Libération du Québec) was holding meetings. Following the recommendations of the commission, Security Services were removed from the jurisdiction of the RCMP. At no time did the Force relinquish this responsibility voluntarily. It was arbitrarily removed, and CSIS (Canadian Security Intelligence Service) was formed in 1984.

In the 1980s, the federal government decided that the RCMP commissioner would become part of the government as a deputy minister. This was perhaps the single worst management decision to have been made by government regarding the RCMP. Objectivity has been lost, and independence from the federal government of the day has been subverted. The commissioner must now deal with another level of bureaucracy, which involves adhering to government regulations and participating in social justice experiments such as recruiting quotas for women and visible minorities, as well as being encumbered by federal policies on hiring and firing. This lack of independence means that decisions are not always made based on the Force's identified needs.

In December 2007, the Task Force on Governance and Cultural Change in the RCMP, chaired by David Brown, QC, released a report that recommended 49 internal changes. Even so, there are few executives at the upper echelon of the RCMP or any politicians who have focused on the essential problem: multijurisdictional saturation. Instead, lofty policy statements and a "Change Management Team" appointed by management speak of elevating professionalism, improving the management environment and tasking individual members to "meet the challenge." Meanwhile, RCMP detachments across the country are overstressed daily and under pressure to do more with less.

With advances in computer technology there has been considerable experimentation with command decentralization. Subdivisions have been expanded into districts, which generally divide provinces in half. The results of these changes have yet to be proven, but it is clear that the Force is still struggling to find the most effective organizational structures.

In recent years the sterling reputation of the Force has been sullied badly. The 2007 tasering death of Polish immigrant Robert Dziekanski at Vancouver International Airport and revelations made at the subsequent Braidwood Inquiry into the tragic incident have been a searing scandal for the RCMP and the beginning of a litany of discrediting incidents that have soiled the name of the Force. Too many examples of professional misconduct, particularly in the province of BC, are leading many Canadians to feel that the RCMP is in need of radical realignment.

The treatment of women within the Force has also been the subject of much scrutiny. The organization I joined was male dominated, and my working life with policewomen was confined to supervising and managing in the latter part of my career. Perhaps my intuition failed me, but I did not detect abuse of female members in the workplace. In fairness to the RCMP, women are still finding their way in the profession, even in police forces that have had women in their ranks for generations. It has taken time for women to carve their own place in the bizarre world of law enforcement, and many of them have been subject to suggestive and even insulting language. Those who survive the tough "battlefield" police environment possess the skills to cope verbally, often humorously, or by demanding change from their work partners. I have witnessed women doing so and receiving a positive and respectful response.

Like many other police and paramilitary organizations, the RCMP still struggles with creating a respectful and safe workplace for women. Allegations of harassment have been made, and a significant number of former female members have joined a class action suit filed in March 2012. It is entirely possible that allegations made in the class-action suit will be substantiated. When I recall members who "stuck the needle in" and harassed me because of my height, it would not be a stretch to assume these same people would enjoy making women feel uncomfortable—and there is little doubt that others have used rank and seniority to sexually exploit women in subordinate positions. Men have been bullied in the Force since 1873, but it was clearly not "macho" to whine to someone about harassment, and it was certainly not advantageous to one's career to be labelled a complainer. To their credit, women are identifying those who harass them in the workplace and are taking them to task. The vast majority of men in the Force will thank them for it.

It is vital to observe that every day thousands of RCMP members carry out their duties professionally, without fear, favour or affection. But if something does not change, the misconduct of a minority will no doubt occur more frequently. Morale is not improving, and members are feeling more and more under siege, both inwardly and outwardly. Current training facilities are not keeping pace with the needs of municipal and provincial contracts, let alone requirements at the federal level. A new commissioner, Bob Paulson, was appointed in 2011, but the mountain that has been left for him to climb may be too high.

Sadly, the Force seems headed for the cliff. One is also reminded of the story of the emperor's new clothes. As he rode through the streets naked, not a single citizen of the kingdom dared to comment. The problem of mandate overload is massive and obvious, yet until the publication of former RCMP member Robert Lunney's 2012 book, *Parting Shots*, few warnings had been voiced. As Lunney states, "Being all things to all people is not an organizational strategy." The Force now has so many diversified and complex tasks at so many levels that success is becoming more and more elusive. Immediate action must be taken to extricate the Force from municipal and provincial policing, despite contract renewals with the provinces that now extend to 2032.

The provinces should be given a fixed period to establish their own police forces, and the RCMP must make a measured transition to an exclusively federal focus, serving also as a support agency to interprovincial crime. The urgency is such that some immediate, tangible action must take the form of the RCMP vacating all of the large municipal contracts in the Lower Mainland of British Columbia. When a vessel is wallowing in heavy seas, a competent captain will jettison cargo to lighten the load in the hope of saving the ship. The commissioner must make a similar decision to rescue his ship. This action would free up considerable human resources that might be redistributed to those parts of the country that are crying out for relief. While not the ultimate solution, such action would ease the load and alleviate current untenable stress and pressure. The RCMP could then bring its considerable expertise to bear primarily on federal responsibilities, assisting provincial and municipal police forces on serious and interprovincial crime when called upon to do so. Rather than being distracted by a myriad of assorted demands, the Force should target national issues such as biker gangs, terrorism and corporate and economic crime along with other criminal maladies at the national level. Should this fail to occur, the mistakes and scandals will continue. It is entirely possible that this Canadian legend may be so discredited that, like the disgraced Canadian Airborne Regiment, it will be disbanded to be replaced by a brand-new entity as Canada's federal police force.

Unwittingly, the Force may be about to encounter their own "perfect storm." What prime minister would risk suffering the wrath of voters in every province but two if he endorses the removal of the RCMP from their provincial and municipal duties? Surely it would be politically wiser to allow the organization to continue to discredit itself until it is viewed as incapable of effectively offering a viable service. If this venerable Canadian icon is not thrown a lifeline of sorts, its eventual demise is inevitable.

It will cause nationwide trauma if the RCMP is not saved from destruction. It is a long-revered Canadian icon, etched indelibly into our country's psyche. Canada's leaders have a responsibility to ensure this national treasure is preserved. The Royal Canadian Mounted Police is still admired worldwide. Canada will be a smaller country without it.

Turning the herd will not be an easy task. The logistics are difficult and complex, and resistance to change will be rampant. It will take great political courage, stamina and dynamic leadership. If current leaders both inside and outside the Force do not move on these initiatives, the disasters will continue. The RCMP will be crippled by a barrage of criticism and found broken and dying at the bottom of the cliff.

ACKNOWLEDGEMENTS

My most sincere thanks go out to my first senior constable, William Joseph McCoy, and to Gerald Scholefield, Ron Mangan, George Apps, Larry Knight, Clyde Kitteringham and Danny Bereza for their insights, mentoring and friendship while I cobbled the work together. Without their input, the project might have died on the order table. I'd also like to thank Ken Crosby's wife, Betty, for permission to use Ken's poem, "Last Post." And I will never forget Alice, the "life saver" from Moose Jaw.

A writer will never be an author without two essential individuals: a publisher and an editor. I had the epitome of both. My gratitude forever goes out to Rodger Touchie and my editor, Lesley Reynolds; Lara Kordic, a most wonderful copy editor; and Kate Scallion, who, at the outset, gave me encouragement when I needed it most; Jacqui Thomas, who created the design; and Susan Adamson who did the layout. And my final words go out to my soulmate and wife of 25 years. Lynne, you are my inspiration, my light, my sounding board. Without your nurturing and anchoring skills, this book would have never happened.

In Memory of:
Sandy Ashby, née Roach
Joan Dooley, née Hollett

ABOUT THE AUTHOR

Ian Parsons was born in Kamsack, Saskatchewan. Formally trained as a musician, he joined the Lord Strathcona's Horse Regimental Band in Calgary Alberta, and in 1961 he joined the RCMP. During his 33 years with the force, he served in many capacities, including as an academic instructor, researcher, management trainer and commissioner officer. He has worked in Alberta, Saskatchewan, Ontario, Newfoundland, Manitoba and British Columbia. Ian has a BA from Carleton University, majoring in psychology and law, and holds certificates in general and advanced police studies from the Canadian Police College.

In retirement, Ian has returned to his first love, making music. Together with Danny Bereza, an old friend and fellow musician from the Northernairs dance band in Whitehorse, he plays professionally at bistros in and around the Comox Valley in a duo called Silk Pajamas. Ian lives in Courtenay, BC.